# THE STRAIGHTFORWARD INTERNET

# THE STRAIGHTFORWARD INTERNET

## YOUR SIMPLIFIED GUIDE TO EXPLORING EVERYTHING FROM BASICS TO SOCIAL MEDIA TO THE DEEP WEB

# TERRY LYNNE HALE

**The Straightforward Internet by Terry Lynne Hale**

*Your Simplified Guide to Exploring Everything from Basics to Social Media to the Deep Web*

# CONTENTS

## SECTION 1 - BEGINNING THE VOYAGE TO CYBERSPACE

## SECTION 2 – INTERMEDIATE EXPLORATION

# SECTION 3 – ADVANCED FLIGHT ON THE RAGGEDY EDGE

# SECTION 4: GLOSSARY, REFERENCES AND SITES OF INTEREST

# SECTION 1 - BEGINNING THE VOYAGE TO CYBERSPACE

*This is just the beginning, the beginning of understanding that cyberspace has no limits, no boundaries.*

– Nicholas Negroponte, Greek-American Architect and
Co-founder of MIT's Media Lab

http://www.brainyquote.com/quotes/quotes/n/nicholasne381691.html

# CHAPTER 1
# An Introduction to Cyberspace

## 1A. - What is the Cyberspace?

For most of us who were around during the birth of the Internet, we sure never dreamed it would become this big and this universal. The Internet is no longer just a convenient way to get messages or buy things on line. It's become a universe all its own.

In that weird way that art sometimes mimics life, think of the *Back to the Future* trilogy. When most of us first saw those movies, we were probably pretty amazed by some of the things they thought the future would provide. Handheld tablet computers, movies with 3D signs, video conferencing, shoot, even TV glasses were all kind of amazing to us back then. And now, they're part of our everyday lives.

Well, except hover boards. They never did figure out how to make those. I have to say, I'd be far more interested in owning one of those that I would a pair of sneakers that lace themselves. Thanks anyway Nike.

Despite the fact that those *Back to the Future* props seemed impossible in the 1980s, they're possible now. Computers made them possible.

Of course, the movie didn't get everything right. In their future, their main form of communication came via fax machine. When was the last time you really needed a fax machine? We have virtual ones, tied into our email. Many of us haven't fought with a "paper Jam" or "PC load letter" error in at least ten years.

So Back to the Future got a few things right about the future, but they never could have predicted how truly awesome October 21, 2015 would be.

Minus hover boards.

The goal of this book is to give you a widely rounded view of the new digital universe we're living in, from simple email all the way to the dark side of the deep web. No matter your level of understanding, whether you're a relative newb (don't worry, we'll get into online acronyms later) , or pretty advanced in flying the digital universe, you're sure to find something new to learn in here.

The Internet levels the playing field for all of us. Young and old, novice or expert, all the information you need to navigate this digital universe is right at your fingertips. The first step is understanding the Internet of things. Also known as IoT.

You might have heard that phrase 'Internet of things' thrown around a lot these days, without really knowing what it is. In reality, it's nothing more than showing us how we're all connected to the World Wide Web. Remember the game the Six Degrees of Kevin Bacon? Well, consider the Internet of things the One Degree of Cyberspace, because these days, most of us are only one degree of separation from the Internet.

Chances are, you're already connected. Even if you don't have a computer at home, you might have a smartphone, or a tablet, or something else that gets Wi-Fi service. You might even have a smart TV with Wi-Fi in it. Pretty much any piece of complex technology you can buy these days has a wireless connection and some way of connecting to the Internet.

Not everyone that has invested in a "connected car" truly understands what a connected car means to life as they knew it. The first time they get an email from the car, advising it needs an oil change, their heart might stop. *I immediately assumed that it was possessed, much like that infamous Plymouth, Christine.*

Luckily, a tech savvy friend told me what was going on before I hired an exorcist.

The Internet of Things is just what it sounds like. The Internet is creeping into everything, from our phones, all the way to our cars and houses. It's estimated that by 2020, there will be 4.9 billion Internet connected things in use[1]. Some of those things haven't been invented yet. They might not have even been imagined yet.

Navigating the Internet is no longer optional. It's a necessity. Whether you know it or not, chances are you're already using it a lot more than you think. Your bank uses it for electronic transfer, your employer probably uses it to clock your hours. You might already be using it for paying your bills.

By the end of this book, you'll know all the basics of using the Internet of Things, as well as a few more advanced things. You'll know everything you need to know about finding information, socializing, sending messages, using online auctions and even about delving into the deep web. Regardless of what you're looking for, you'll know how to get there.

The time has come for you to immerse yourself in it. It's already all around you. Let's learn how to navigate this new digital universe, without worrying about roads. Because surely you remember what Doc said about roads?

# 1B. - How it Works

Whether you're a Doc, who wants to know the inner workings of everything, or a Marty, who just wants to have some fun, understanding the basics of how it's designed and where it came from is always a good place to start.

The Internet originally started as part of the United States Pentagon's formation of ARPA (Advanced Research Projects Agency) in 1957. This group created something called Arpanet, which was a program that some believe was designed to survive a nuclear attack. In 1969, Arpanet was expanded upon, by the group adding a fourth node, or processing location/connection point. More wouldn't be done with it until 1989, when, SCNet or National Science Foundation Network replaced Arpanet, expanding upon its abilities as a network for sharing info.

One thing to note is that there are many competing origin theories about the Internet. However, regardless of whether you believe that it was for military purposes or research, it was never supposed to be for the general public. Even the people who built the earliest versions had no idea what they were building. It was mainly developed with the intention of communicating between computers, but I doubt anyone at the time could have pictured how important it would become today.

So rather than go with the science, I'm going to stick to the basics. The Internet is made up of two types of computers: SERVERS (which store pictures, information, and all kinds of data) and CLIENTS which is what our personal computers are. Think of a SERVER as "serving" the information to us when we request it.

Today, the Internet is a communications tool for every user, sharing multimedia experiences, information and ideas. The Web connects one Internet site to another through hypertext links. In the early 1990s, the commercial sector's sales and marketing departments discovered the astronomical (mind-blowing) reach the Internet provides. Today, for-profit as well as not-for-profit companies rely on the Internet to interact with their customers or contributors worldwide.

For critics out there, know that the Internet is distinct from the World Wide Web. Email and newsgroups are not part of the World Wide Web. But, without the WWW, the Internet wouldn't be useful to most people because of its complex technology. Hypertext links connect one Internet website to another. They appear as highlighted text (often a different color from the rest) and if you click on the link, you are taken to another page. Sometimes a new window opens up but often you find yourself on a site completely unrelated to what you were looking for to begin with.

While the World Wide Web, cyberspace, the Internet, etc. are all actually different things, they're so closely connected that I'm going to go ahead and use the terms interchangeably through this book. After all, when it comes to the net, there really aren't any rules. No one regulating agency exists to make sure certain things don't get on the net. That's the good and the bad of the Internet.

**The good? Anyone can say anything.**

**The bad? Anyone can say anything.**

Mitchell Kapor, a pioneer in the personal computing industry, entrepreneur and software designer said: *Getting information off the Internet is like taking a drink from a fire hydrant.*

http://en.thinkexist.com/quotation/getting_information_off_the_internet_is_like/216131.html

The amount of people using the Internet changes daily, with new users showing up, and new websites going up, every single day. According to the June 30, 2015 Internet World Stats (www.Internetworldstats.com), the estimated world population in 2015 is 7,260,621,118. Of this number, 3,270,490,584 people use the Internet. In North America alone, 87.9% of population use the Internet![2]

Cyberspace is limitless. It will never get too crowded for someone else to jump in. If fact, every time someone signs on, it just gets bigger. Of course, the problem with that is that it can make it a bit difficult to find things. Much like time traveling in the DeLorean, you need to know where you're going before you get there.

# 1C. - What's There to do in Cyberspace?

Cyberspace is its own universe and because of that, you can do just about anything there that you could do in real life. You can:

**Work** – Everyone has their own individual experiences and those experiences can often be used to make money. The term professional blogger was something that didn't exist 20 years ago, and now it's a consistently growing career field. Sites like http://www.blogger.com and https://wordpress.com/ will even allow you to start your own blogging career for free. If you have a heavy interest in politics, a great well known blog to get into is http://www.huffingtonpost.com Or you can set up your own storefront on a site like https://www.etsy.com/ or http://eBay.com/ to sell your products. There's virtually no end to the businesses you can create on the Internet.

**Find love** – About 20% of relationships now start online[3]. 20%! Turns out Doc would have never had to go back to the Old West to find a lady if online dating had been big in his day. In addition, these online dating sites run the gamut of niches, for people who are looking to date within their own religious groups, to dating sites that are just for golfers, and more. Chances are, whatever your interest, you can find a specialty online dating site that caters to it.

**Travel** – Did you miss the Louvre in Paris because of the ridiculous line? That's ok, you can take an online tour from the comfort of your living room. Just go to http://www.louvre.fr/en/visites-en-ligne. You can go to museums you never thought possible, or even get a ton of knowledge to use before you take a real life trip. For instance, did you know that you can't wear a tank top in Vatican City? You do now. I've never been to the Vatican, but now I know if I ever go, to bring a sweater thanks to the Vatican's website!

**Learn** – No matter what you're curious about, you can find anything and everything under the sun. If you don't have time to travel for school, there are a ton of accredited universities online that you can take classes from. Or you can just get those questions you always wanted answered, answered! Somebody knows and chances are, they've shared their knowledge online.

Regardless of what you want to do, whether you want to learn about the fall of the Roman Empire, or just order a pizza, you can do it with the Internet. It is the invisible universe all around us and there is nowhere you can't get to with it.

It's your DeLorean for the ride. Whether you want to go back in time by reading up on the history of Tombstone, or head on into the future by taking a virtual ride in one of Google's driverless cars, you can do it. The universe is wide open to you. Enjoy it.

# 1D. - What Is Downloading And What Is Uploading?

In the simplest term, when you're downloading something, you're receiving it. If someone sends you a file to open, you're downloading that file. For uploading, you're sending a file away from you. All those selfies you see on Twitter? People are uploading those to another site.

For how it's transferred, you're looking at something called File Transfer Protocol, or FTP. FTP is pretty much built into most browsers, like Internet Explorer and Firefox, but there are also many freely downloadable FTP utilities as well. Yup, you can download something to make downloading easier!

I'm not going to delve too deeply into how to download, because that's computer vs. Internet basics. However, there's a lot written on the basics of computers that cover everything from choosing your computer, to using special programs. A few good books for beginners include:

*Absolute Beginners Guide to Computer Basics* (5th Edition) by Michael Miller

*Is This Thing On? A Late Bloomers Computer Handbook* by Abigail Stokes.

One thing to note about downloading is that if you don't do it carefully, it's a pretty darn good way to get yourself a virus. While I'll go over that in more detail later, it's important to remember that the common cause of viruses is unsafe downloads.

Before you download anything, even if you've run a virus scan on the file, do yourself a favor and search the file name on the Internet. Search the actual file name -- there are a lot of copycat freeware's out there that use popular software names to trick you into downloading Malware or Adware. Both can be really tricky to get rid of. It's much easier to avoid viruses than it is to get rid of one that has already infected your computer.

When you start a download, you'll often get a popup window that asks "Do you want to run file.exe".

The exe on the end means it's an executable file. It means it's going to make your computer do something and it might not be something you want it to do.

Before you click "ok" take a minute and search that file on the Internet. For instance, recently, I downloaded a new stopwatch program to a computer. At least, I thought I was. Then, the computer said "Do you want to run optimize.exe?".

That didn't sound right, so I searched exactly what optimize.exe is. The search led to a site that indicated that not only was this not the file I wanted, it was actually pornographic adware that is nearly impossible to get rid of once you install it.

Before you download something, especially something that's an exe file, do your due diligence. Never open attachments from someone you don't know and never download an executable file without thoroughly checking it online first.

# 1E. - How We Travel

The DeLorean required enough energy to power a nuclear bomb to operate, but luckily, the Internet is a bit more user (and NSA) friendly. We don't need plutonium for that. All we need is an Internet Service Provider, or ISP.

Depending on what ISP you use, we'll get a slower or faster connection. I'm going to start describing the slowest and work my way to the fastest.

**Dial UP –** We probably all remember that screeching, tonal sound that initially indicated our Internet was hooking up. I remember. It's not a pleasant noise. The original option for Internet connectivity was run through phone lines and sent info to and from the computer via a modem. Using it would tie up your phone line, meaning you either had to choose between the Internet and getting your phone calls. Typical dial up- speeds can range from 2400 bps to 56 Kbs per second, which isn't that fast. Using dial up would be virtually impossible if you wanted to do things like stream movies. In fact, it's so slow that only about 2% of people still use it.[4]

Others have moved onto much faster options like Cable and DSL.

**DSL –** DSL also uses a telephone line for connection, but in a different way. It's short for Digital Subscriber Line and uses a specific area of your phone line to send and receive information. Because of this, it's always on and you can still use your phone when you're on it. It takes up unused frequencies in your phone line, allowing you to transmit and review information faster. This ISP requires a phone line, a filter and a sending/receiving box that translates data. These speeds are much faster, ranging from 1 Mbps to 3.0 Mbps on average.

**Satellite –** Satellite is a lesser used ISP, as it's generally for rural areas that don't have access to companies that provide cable or DSL. Chances are, if you're using it, you know it, because you have to have a Satellite dish to use it. Speed can vary widely, from something comparable to dial up speeds, all the way to 50 Mbps for higher tech systems. It's frequently used as a service of last resort, when no other services are available, as set-up can be quite expensive.

**Wireless or Wi-Fi –** This is another popular Internet service provider that again, is always on and doesn't interrupt a phone line. It requires some hardware to set up initially, and is usually created as a password protected network. You might have heard the term Wi-Fi hotspot before, or free Wi-Fi and that's generally a system a business (like Starbucks) keeps open for customers to use. If your computer has Wi-Fi capabilities, and it probably will if made in the past 10 years, you can use it.

**3G/4G/4G LTE –** If you have a smartphone, you'll probably see that on there. They're short for 3rd generation, fourth generation, and fourth generation long term evolution respectively. This is the wireless protocol that comes through your cellphone and uses your specific cellular network for transmitting info. 5G is within sight.

**Cable –** Cable is currently the fastest of all connection speeds. This ISP method provides service through the same coax cable as is used for your cable TV service. It requires a modem. It is always on, no waiting and you have full use of your telephone line. The connection speed can be affected by the number of local subscribers online at the same time. Speeds often range anywhere from 3.0Mbps (55x faster than dial-up) to 6.0Mbps (100x faster than dial up).

Of course, aside from the cost of equipment, you can generally assume that the faster your speed, the higher your monthly cost of Internet service will be. The only exception to this is Wi-Fi, and if you know a friendly neighborhood business, you can generally do your Internet surfing for free. (Keep in mind, this option isn't terribly secure, as I will cover more fully later.) Depending on what you want to do, and your budget, you'll need to consider your speed. If you're like me and you're a heavy Internet user, who is using the Internet as a cable replacement, you'll want to go with the fastest possible connection your area has to offer.

Then, somewhere in all of this is FIBER. Unlike the others requiring electricity and/or copper, fiber uses light that transmits through clear glass or plastic cables.

# CHAPTER 2
## Introduction to Electronic Communication

## 2A. - Introduction to Email

One of the most common methods of electronic communication is email. That's certainly one thing *Back to the Future* didn't predict. They thought we'd all be carrying around portable fax machines! With email, you can instantly send letters, files, photos and even faxes with certain add on programs. Email is a necessary part of our daily lives, with one third of Americans checking theirs upwards of 150 times per day![5]

It's hard to think of a time where there wasn't email. The earliest instance actually happened back in 1971, when a computer engineer named Ray Tomlinson wanted to find a way of sending messages between different computers[6]. However, Ray had a problem. He needed to find a numerical value that couldn't possibly be found in someone's name. After giving it only a few seconds of thought, he chose the @ symbol. It's funny that a decision that took only a minute to decide would come to affect our lives in so many ways.

First, and most basic, you can have both an email and an email client. Your email address is one individual site, while your email client, available from your desktop, is a place where you can add all your various emails to check them at once. Your email client will also often be where you'll keep your appointment calendar.

I highly recommend using an email client rather than just checking each individual email address every single day. It saves time and effort, plus can be used on a mobile device so you can get your email on the go.

Some of the more popular email clients by market share, outside of mobile, include[7];

- Microsoft Outlook        20.14%
- Outlook.com              13.57%
- Apple Mail               11%
- Gmail                    8.43%
- Windows Live Desktop     2.34%
- Thunderbird              1.03%
- AOL                      0.91%

For your mobile, generally it's better to just go with the default one that comes as part of your phone's operating system. It's already set up to integrate all your email addresses, so all you have to do is sign in and go.

You're probably well versed in the basics of sending an email, receiving it and clearing out your spam; but here are some other fun and useful things you can do with email in order to make the most of your electronic communication.

- **Use your Email for Faxing** – With programs like eFax available out there, you can easily replace outdated fax machines with a simple scanner and email. http://www.efax.com/ is a popular option and is easy to incorporate into most standard email programs.

- **Send an eCard** – There are lots of great sites for sending eCards. https://www.hallmarkecards.com/ is one that allows you to send them and http://www.123greetings.com/ is another popular option. For even more innovative greetings, check out JacquieLawson.com

- **Set up stationery** – If you really want to personalize your email, setting up your background to a specific stationery can be a fun choice. You can usually find stationery options under the settings menu. You can also change your default font and color there as well.

- **Block users** – Whether you're dealing with a persistent spammer, or just someone you'd rather not deal with on a regular basis, you can easily block them as long as you have the email

address or name. Again, this will often be an option under your settings menu.

- **Prioritize your to-do list** – With the flagging option in your email client, you can flag emails for importance, so you know you need to follow up later. Simply click on the flag in the (usually) right hand corner of your email and that will flag it as an important email.

- **Get Organized** – With the folders option in your email, you can add new folders to your account in order to create a designated folder for all your special files. While how you do this will change client by client, generally you can do this from the settings menu as well.

Now when it comes do doing these specialty settings, it usually needs to be done from the actual email you use, as opposed to your email client. Most email clients have been pared down significantly these days, in order to make them more mobile friendly, so doing advanced things like blocking, adding folders or customizing your messages should be done from your actual email account. For the most part, it's easy to figure out how to do if the options aren't available on your setting menu. The instructions can vary widely from program to program, so below is a listing of major email providers with links to their 'how to' and help pages.

- **Gmail** - https://support.google.com/mail/#topic=3394144

- **Outlook/Hotmail** - http://windows.microsoft.com/en-us/windows/outlook-help

- **AOL** - https://help.aol.com/products/aol-mail

- **Yahoo! Mail** - https://help.yahoo.com/kb/mail

- **Mail.com** - https://help.mail.com/en/

- **Yandex** - https://yandex.com/support/mail/

## 2B. – Introduction to Instant Messaging

Instant messaging is a popular form of communication that many people are now using as much, and sometimes even more, than email. This type of messaging allows you to reply quickly and in real time, so you can chat with someone you haven't seen in a while or get ahold of someone quickly.

Just about every social network or email program has its own instant messaging feature, and they generally come with these options;

- **Chat** – Chat allows you to add people who are your friends or contacts to a list and chat with them all at once, or one at a time, for sending quick real time messages.

- **Attachments** – You can also send pretty much any kind of file, as long as it isn't too big, like photos, videos, documents and more.

- **Talk** – Many chat programs come with an option to actually talk to your friends over the Internet, using your computers mic and speakers, rather than a telephone. The quality of these calls will change based on your own connection speed and the programs capabilities.

- **Video Chat** – Certain chat programs like Skype and Facetime will allow

you to have a real time video chat with people on your list. Again, the quality of this feature will depend on your own computer's capabilities.

- **Mobile** – Just about any instant message program you can think of has mobile compatibility, meaning you can download it as an app to your phone and use it there. Some chat programs will only have some features available, while others will allow all the features of their program to be used on a mobile device.

Most instant message programs are free, and can be downloaded as an app, or on your desktop. Globally, some of the most popular Instant Messaging programs are;[8]

- **WhatsApp** – 800 million users

- **Facebook Messenger** – 700 million users

- **QQ Mobile** – 603 million users

- **WeChat** – 600 million users

- **Skype** – 300 million users

- **Viber** – 249 million users

Instant Messaging is a very popular form of communication, as it's faster than email and allows you to do generally the same things as with email. However, there is another form of online communication that is gaining popularity: ephemeral messaging.

## 2C. – Introduction to Ephemeral Messaging

Ephemeral messaging is similar to instant messaging, with one major difference. Ephemeral messages are designed to disappear.

Why would you want your messages to disappear? Maybe you sent a regrettable one after too many drinks. Maybe you sent a naughty snap to your significant other. Either way, with ephemeral messaging, the program is designed to allow you to open the message, gives you a limited time to read it, and then it disappears. It was designed this way because of those regrettable drunk-and-texts that so many college students hate themselves for sending.

Take one of the most popular ephemeral messaging aps, Snapchat. This app was developed at Stanford University, when three college students Evan Spiegel, Reggie Brown, and Bobby Murphy were talking about one of them sending regrettable messages to a girl he liked[9]. After Brown said "we wish the photos we sent would just disappear" the three came up with a billion dollar idea. After all, Brown wasn't alone. There were plenty of college students who, despite having heard the warning, "once you send something on the Internet, it's there forever" still sent things that they wished would disappear.

Hey, everyone's dumb in college. It's a rite of passage.

But those three college kids did a very smart thing. They created a messaging program designed to make people's message disappear. Snapchat was born and caught on like wild fire. When it comes to ephemeral messaging programs, Snapchat is probably the most well-known, but other programs like Frankly and ArmorChat are gaining popularity as well.

One thing to note about these ephemeral messaging programs is that they aren't all foolproof. Tech savvy message receivers can often find other ways to screenshot the messages and save them, though ephemeral message developers are finding ways to work around these problems.

## 2D. - Etiquette and Netiquette

Electronic communication etiquette, or netiquette, can change from one year to the next, however some basics remain the same. Here are a few things you should always keep in mind for email;

• **No all CAPS –** I'm sure you've heard this before, but all CAPs is yelling. As you shouldn't be sending flame emails in the first place, there's no need to yell. Which brings us to number 2.

• **Watch your tone –** Sarcasm doesn't translate well in email, and can come off as gruff. Avoid it when possible and avoid misunderstandings.

- **Reply all sparingly –** If everyone on the list doesn't need to see your reply, then don't used reply all. Especially don't use it just to say 'thanks' or 'got it'. Also, when everyone else is replying all, and you reply all to tell *them* not to reply all, you're just as bad as them.

- **Know when to emoji –** Emoticons or emojis can be a lot of fun, but don't always offer the most professional look. When emailing friends or family, they might be fine. However, when emailing a resume or professional correspondence, they're best avoided. A good rule of thumb is to not use an emoji until after the other person has first. The same goes for acronyms like 'lol'. They work ok in instant messages, or any time when space is limited, but might not always be appropriate in email.

- **Avoid fancy fonts and light colors –** While that script font might look pretty, it can also be pretty darn unreadable. Same goes for light colors. Even if it looks all all right to you, display can vary widely from device to device, making that simple message you sent virtually unreadable.

- **Be mindful of time –** While I don't necessarily agree with this one, sometimes sending a message at 3 in the morning can send the wrong idea. If you don't have to send the message at 3 am, you may not want to. (I get some of my best work done then..)

- **Don't forward chain mail –** This etiquette tip is actually such a major problem that it really deserves its own section.

## 2E. - About Chain Mail

We all get them. Those messages forwarded from a friend or relative that says "send this message to 50 people and you'll find your true love tonight" or some other equally unlikely thing. Let's make this clear. There has never been one instance of someone finding their true love or making their first million because they forwarded a piece of chain mail.

The history is actually a bit more nefarious than that. The goal of chain mail is to make its way to as many people as possible. One thing scammers, hackers and social engineers know is that it is the best way to both get mass emails in bulk, and it's a good way to spread a virus rapidly. Chain mail is not lucky and no one wants to get it. At best, you're just annoying your friends by sending them unnecessary emails. At worst, you're infecting them with a virus.

Of course, not all chain mails are as obvious. Some might include a funny video or story. However, the goal of that mail could be the same as any other piece of chainmail, with the goal of getting emails or sending viruses. As a result, even if you think it's the funniest thing you've ever seen, don't forward it. If you don't know the origin of the attachment or email, just delete it.

But what about if you get an urgent email that you think needs to be forwarded to people? What if you get an email about a missing child or some criminal activity to watch out for? Before you click forward, do your homework with a little bit of fact checking.

## 2F. - Fact Checking on the Internet

We've all seen posts on Facebook, or gotten emails forwarded to us that give people a warning horror story about something awful that happened, that the police want people to be aware of.

Take this story, as an example.

*At a petrol pump, a man came over and offered his services as a painter to a lady filling petrol in her car and left his visiting card. She said nothing but accepted his card out of sheer kindness and got into the car. The man then got into a car driven by another person.*

*As the lady left the service station, she saw the men following her out of the station at the same time. Almost immediately, she started to feel dizzy and could not catch her breath. She tried to open the window and realized that the odor was on her hand; the same hand with which she had received the card from the person at the service station.*

*She then noticed the men were immediately behind her and she felt she needed to do something at that moment. She drove into the first driveway and began to honk her horn repeatedly to ask for help. The men drove away but the lady still felt pretty bad for several minutes after she could finally catch her breath. Apparently, there was a substance on the card that could have seriously injured her.*

*This drug is called 'BURUNDANGA'. (Not known To People So Far but sufficient Information Is available in the Net) and it is used by people who wish to incapacitate a victim in order to steal from or take advantage of them. This drug is four times more dangerous than the date rape drug and is transferable on a simple card or paper. So please take heed and make sure you don't accept cards when you are alone or from someone on the streets. This applies to those making house calls and slipping you a card when they offer their services*[10].

That message was originally seen in an email in 2008. It sounds pretty terrifying and plays on our worst fears, that doing something as simple as taking a business card from someone could result in us becoming the victim of a crime. Of course if we receive this email, we want to forward it to everyone we know, so they know not to take business cards from strangers.

The problem is this email is fake. Nothing like the above story has ever happened. While the drug burundanga does exist, it does not work in the way described in the above story and has never been reported as being used in any kind of attack like the one in the story.

How do I know this? A simple search of Snopes. Snopes is an Internet fact checking site that looks into many email hoaxes. They're constantly updating their database with new stories they've debunked after doing thorough research.

To check out Snopes and stay up to date on the latest cyber hoaxes, go here: http://www.snopes.com/

Before you forward something like that, fact check. Check Snopes, or if the message is claiming that it's a release from a police department, check the police department's website. Above all, take any message you receive with a grain of salt. If it's filled with spelling or grammatical errors, chances are it did not come from a government agency. Remember what was said in Chapter 1. The good and bad of the Internet; anyone can say anything.

# 2G. - Avoiding Viruses

Even the best of us get hit with a nasty virus now and then. Most of the computer and mobile phone infections we get come from human error, from us not being careful enough when we check our email. In order to avoid getting viruses, it's best to obey the following rules.

1. Don't open emails from anyone you don't know.

2. Don't open attachments you didn't ask for.

3. Don't follow unsolicited links.

4. If the email is from someone you know, but the subject line is strange like "buy discount Viagra' etc., don't open it. Chances are one of your friends got hacked.

5. In chat programs, don't accept friend requests from people you don't know.

Generally, if you follow the above rules, which mainly boil down to that age old adage "don't talk to strangers" you'll be just fine. However, sometimes all the due diligence in the world can't stop you from getting hacked.

How do you know when you've been a victim?

In the warnings, I pointed out how even if the email is from a friend, if the subject line is strange, don't open it. One of the best ways that spammers and scammers get people to open emails and spread their viruses is by posing as someone they know. This usually happens when someone opens an email they shouldn't or follows a link.

Usually, these emails will include something called a tracking cookie, which is designed to track your keystrokes so scammers can get into your email. Once they're in, they'll use your email to send their messages. Here's how to know you've been a victim;

1. Your sent folder includes emails you didn't send.

2. You're getting tons of 'failed delivery' message notices.

3. Your account folders have been deleted.

4. You're asked to pass an image challenge during sign in.

5. Your email signature includes a link you never put there.

6. You're getting messages from friends about a strange email you sent.

If this happens, it's generally a sign that your email is compromised. When that happens, you should change your email password immediately and make sure that the 'save my password' box is not checked when you enter it. Double check your personal settings on your email to make sure the hacker hasn't added anything, and finally, scan your computer with your virus software to find and isolate any viruses.

Sometimes, someone might tell you that they've been getting messages from you, but it doesn't appear that the account was compromised. In this case, it's usually a result of spoofing, not hacking, which can be a bit harder to combat.

## 2H. - Spoofing Versus Hacking

An easier way that spammers use your email to get people you trust to open it is to spoof it. Email spoofing is simply someone else using a program to spoof your email address and pretend the message is coming from you, when it's not.

There's a huge amount of online programs out there that will make it look like you're sending emails from one address, when you're really not. As a result spoofing can be hard to stop. Spoofers tend to try to use emails from addresses that aren't in use, so to prevent that, close down any email accounts you don't use. Spoofing does not mean your account has been compromised. The spoofer is just using your email by running it through a spoofing program. There's no need to change your password, because they're not in your account. The most you can do is try to get the spoofer's IP (usually found in the message header in the spoofed email) and report it to the ISP.

The best way to prevent spoofing is to not make your email easily accessible. Don't post it in public places and never leave it in an open forum. If you have to post your email, use AT instead of the @ symbol to keep harvesting bots from finding it and using it.

## 2I. - Emojis and Acronyms

Emojis, aka emoticons, have always been popular for adding a bit of personality to your messages. While most programs come with their own smiley menu for inserting, you can also add emojis to your message a number of ways.

The first is the simplest. Simply go to a site like F Symbols (http://fsymbols.com/ ) to get a comprehensive listing of symbols.

Find the emoji you want to use and highlight it. Then, Copy it (Ctrl + c) and Paste it <Ctrl+ v) where you want it to appear in the message body.

Option two is to use the text form of the emoticon. The most common are :) and :(, though there are hundreds more you can make. Check out this site for a comprehensive listing of text emojis you can use http://cool-smileys.com/text-emoticons.

Another thing people are using a lot of these days are acronyms. These are frequently seen in text messages or anywhere where space might be limited, or time is short, like in chat messages. Here are some of the more common ones you'll see, though more are being created every day:

**BTW -** By The Way -or- Bring The Wheelchair

**B4N -** Bye For Now

**BCNU -** Be Seeing You

**BFF -** Best Friends Forever

**FWIW -** For What It's Worth

**GR8 -** Great

**ILY -** we Love You

**IMO –** In My Opinion

**IMHO -** In My Humble Opinion

**IRL -** In Real Life

**ISO -** In Search Of

**J/K -** Just Kidding

**L8R -** Later

**LMAO -** Laughing My Ass Off

**LOL -** Laugh Out Loud

**NIMBY -** Not In My Back Yard

**NP -** No Problem (sometimes 'nosy parents' for teen texters trying to alert friends that their parents are over their shoulder)

**NUB -** New person to a site or game

**OIC -** Oh, we See

**OMG -** Oh My God

**OT -** Off Topic

**POV -** Point Of View

**ROTFLMAO -** Rolling On The Floor Laughing My Ass Off

**RT -** Real Time -or- ReTweet

**THX or TX or THKS -** Thanks

**TLC -** Tender Loving Care

**TMI -** Too Much Information

**TTYL -** Talk To You Later

**TYVM -** Thank You Very Much

**WTF -** What The F***

**WYWH -** Wish You Were Here

I'm sure Marty and Doc could have never predicted how complicated simplifying things would be! We practically need to learn a foreign language when trying to communicate via email, text and chat these days. Luckily, any time you find yourself lost by an acronym, you can easily look it up online. Online communication is one of the first things you'll want to know the ins and outs of when using the Internet, to avoid getting yourself into trouble, or worse, breaking your computer.

That's why Chapter 3 is going to be all about understanding your hardware, and protecting it with the right software.

# SECTION 2 – INTERMEDIATE EXPLORATION

*Do not fear risk. All exploration, all growth is calculated. Without challenge people cannot reach their higher selves. Only if we are willing to walk over the edge can we become winners.*

- unknown

http://thinkexist.com/quotation/do_not_fear_risk-all_exploration-all_growth_is/7204.html

# CHAPTER 3
## A Look at Computers

A lot of people make the mistake of focusing only on the price of their computer or device without considering what they get for what they spend. In order to really know what you're buying, you need to consider the specs behind what you're buying. I'll start off with the simpler, common devices and move from there.

## 3A. - Introduction to Devices

**PC –** A PC is a personal computer that is set up as a desktop. It's not mobile, so it's pretty impractical to pack it up and take it anywhere. In the past, the desktop computer was the only option if you needed to use it all day, all the time. It was especially necessary if you wanted to run a lot of programs when using it. For the most part, when looking at a desktop, other than your budget, you need to consider the following.

**Memory –** Memory refers to the hard disk storage portion of computers. It is your permanent storage for files, programs and software. Most people can go years and never hit the hard memory limit on their computer. Often, when they think they're running low on memory, they're actually running low on RAM, which is a different kind of memory.

**RAM –** RAM is short for Random Access Memory and it's in charge of the temporary memory of your computer. When you get the message that your computer's memory is low, it's usually talking about this, as you have too many applications running and it's taking up your available RAM.

Your memory and RAM work together in managing files on your computer. While the file is open and being edited, or the application is in use, you're using RAM for the memory. However, once it's saved, it's saved to your hard drive, using the hard drive memory.

Most desktop programs these days come standard with around 500 GB of hard drive memory and 4GB of RAM. This is because you need a lot of memory for permanent static storage (hard drive memory), and not quite as much for programs that are running (RAM). Generally, it's the amount of RAM your computer has that will affect the speed at which it runs applications. Well, that and your processor.

**CPU –** Your central processing unit is your computer's brain. It carries out all the instructions you give the computer. The CPU can be an AMD or Intel CPU, though Intel is kind of the gold standard and usually a better choice. These processors will have two to six cores. Consider the cores like the cylinders in the engine of the DeLorean. The more cylinders, the faster it goes. Mainly, the standard these days is the ability to process 62 bits of information (or eight bites) at one time. Again, the more bits, the faster it goes. For exploring your CPU's speed, check out: CPU Benchmark. Keep in mind, there are ads on this site and we're directing you here only for evaluating the processing speed of your current (or potentially new CPU.)

So how much speed do you need for your computer? That depends on what you want to do with it. Let's assume you have the essential programs that most computers need just to be useful. The essentials generally include;

- Microsoft Office (which includes Word, Excel, PowerPoint and more)

  ♦ A free alternative is Apache Open Office

- A media player (for playing videos)

- Adobe (or another PDF Reader)

- Antivirus and Malware Scanning Software

- An Internet Browser (like Google , Chrome, Safari or Firefox)

- Security software

These are the desktop essentials and if you're just planning on doing things like going online, writing documents and checking your email, then you should be fine going with the bare minimum. However, if you're above entry level, a diehard gamer who wants to run programs like Steam, or a person who needs to be able to create videos or other multimedia presentations, you'll want to up your CPU, hard Memory and RAM.

Desktop computers will run you anywhere from $300 to $800 when purchased new. They used to be the go to standard for anyone who was looking for something that would be durable for all day use. However, these days, many people are using laptops not just for travel, but as desktop replacements.

**Laptops –** Laptops have become much more powerful through the years and are quickly replacing desktops as the new all day use computer. Most laptops are now comparable in memory and RAM to desktop computers, and use similar CPUs. What you really need to look for in a laptop is battery life.

If you're not planning on keeping it plugged in, then you'll want a laptop that's able to hold a charge for a while. You'll usually get two different battery lives for a laptop. Both the offline battery life and the online battery life. Offline, you'll consume much less power, but online, your battery might start to go low after only a few hours.

Another thing to consider is portability and screen size. If you travel a lot and take your laptop everywhere, then you might want to go with a smaller screen size to make it easier to carry. If you're planning on using it as a desktop replacement, then you can go with a larger screen. Screens run anywhere from 13" all the way to around 20 inches.

**Netbooks or Mini Notebooks –** These are much smaller options that aren't as powerful as todays ultra-powerful laptops, and aren't suitable as desktop replacements. The battery life is great, because they're very lightweight, but they don't have the speed you need, nor the memory to run constant programs. These are a good choice for people who don't use their computer a lot, or need a lighter alternative for travel. They're also budget friendly, running anywhere from $280 to $430. If you own software you love on CD/DVD, you will need to buy an external disc drive since these units do not come with drives.

**Tablets and Convertible Laptops –** These ultra-portable devices are mainly meant for entertainment, though cloud storage is making them more accessible as working computers. Tablets have virtual or on screen keyboards, while convertibles have detachable keyboards that aren't quite as durable as the keyboard you'd find on a standard laptop or netbook. The big issue with using these constantly is memory capacity and RAM. Your average tablet has about 64 GB of hard memory, and 1 to 3 GB of RAM, making it incapable of working with most programs. However, its lighter size does allow for a longer battery life and cloud storage capabilities are increasing what these cutting edge hybrids can do every single day. You can get one of these devices for anywhere from $150 all the way to around $900 for upper range, more laptop comparable models.

**Smartphones –** This is a mobile computing device just about all of us carry these days. The smartphone is great for quick Internet browsing, playing games and even reading files, but of course, due to its size and storage abilities, can't run most computer based programs without the use of cloud storage. Most smartphones you'll see generally only have about 500 MB of RAM, though luckily, most phone applications consume less than 50MB when in use.

## 3B. - Computer Peripherals and Accessories

There are a wide variety of computer peripherals available now. These pretty much include anything you plug into one of the USB ports on your computer. The most common you'll need in your day to day activities include

- Printer/scanner

- Keyboard

- Mouse

- Web cam (often comes built into many systems these days)

- Speakers/Mic (again often comes built into newer systems)

**Printers –** one of the first considerations you'll deal with when buying a printer is the price. There are printers out there available for as low as $30. Just keep in mind manufacturers of printers often sell their equipment at a loss and make up for it with high cost ink or toner cartridges. Before buying a printer for price, check to see how much that toner cartridge is going to cost you down the road. Often, buying expensive to begin with will save you more money in the long run.

There are various types of printers available, with the most common being Inkjet and laser printers. Injects use droplets of color from one to four cartridges, usually in the primary color family, and print black and white considerably faster than they render color. They are a better choice for printing color photos than laser, which is better for faster, black and white, high volume printing.

Specialty Photo or Snapshot Printers are compact and produce very good quality. These usually print directly from your camera's memory card without needing to be connected to your computer.

Mobile Printers are also called "personal printers" because they're designed for people on the go. Compact, they normally fit right into a briefcase and often have a battery in addition to an external power cord. Memory card readers make it possible to print without a computer.

**Scanners –** Most scanners will come as part of your all-in-one (printer/copier/scanner) type printers, though they can be bought separately if you only need to do a lot of scanning. Scanners are generally the same as printers, in that you can get a high volume one, capable of processing a lot of documents in a short period of time, or a high quality one, better for scanning one at a time at a higher quality.

**Keyboards and mice –** These two go together like Doc and Marty. Most times, they'll come as a bundle, but you can buy one without the other if you need to. While most laptops come with a built in one, some people prefer to hook up a keyboard and separate mouse for ease of use. The biggest makers of these devices include Logitech, ADESA, Microsoft, Unite, Saitek and Cherry.

While it might feel these are all the same, they differ significantly, and not just in price. The cheapest option comes in a wired keyboard and mouse set, with no specialty features, that you can get for under $15 as a combo. However, if you spend a lot of time typing and don't want to deal with the wires,

there are wireless options that you can get for under $20. Wireless options are easy, as all you have to do is plug a small receiver button into your USB. If you get the combo option, they'll often work off of the same USB, saving you a port for other use.

While in the past, Mice used to come standard with a little metal ball in them to mimic movement, now, the vast majority of them are optical, meaning a small laser tracks movement to replicate it on the computer screen. Optical mice are now just as cheap as the old 'ball' mice used to be several years ago.

Keyboards come with more ergonomic options now than ever, though ergonomically designed keyboards cost more in the short term, they might save you money when you don't have to pay for carpal tunnel surgery down the road! Another nice option to have for keyboards is illumination where the keys are backlit, so you can type even during those bouts of insomnia.

**Webcams –** Many computers, both laptop and desktop, come with built in webcams now. If you do buy a webcam to add to your computer, it will often plug into your USB and be of a "plug-and-play" variety, meaning that all the files and drivers needed to run it are transmitted as soon as you plug it in. Often, webcams will come with their own software, but there's tons of software you can get for free for real time chatting. Here are some of the more popular options;

- **Yahoo! Messenger** http://messenger.yahoo.com/

- **Skype** http://www.skype.com

- **Google Chat** http://www.google.com/chat/video

Keep in mind that while you might be able to chat for free, rendering and creating videos will require the addition of another video editing program, like YouCam or Cyber link. A webcam can cost anywhere from under $10, to hundreds of dollars for higher definition cameras with their own video editing software.

**Monitors** – I almost always recommend buying a desktop as an all-in-one package, i.e. your computer comes with the monitor that was created just for it. This way, you won't deal with any connectivity issues. In addition, many companies are developing desktops where everything you need in the computer is inside of the monitor, so this section will soon be obsolete. Typical monitor screens run 19-20" on the smaller scale and 22" – 26" on the larger. Some brand names include Dell, Apple, LG, Acer, View Sonic, Gateway, HP and Sony. You can spend over $100 to several hundred on a good quality monitor.

**Speakers** – Speakers are one of the most frequently sought after items when it comes to computer peripherals as oftentimes, internal speakers don't really pack enough punch. If you're the kind of person who likes streaming their TV or watching YouTube videos, you'll probably want to invest in some better speakers. You can pay anywhere from $10 to $400, depending on what type of quality speakers you're looking for. While all speakers will boost the sounds, more expensive ones will allow you to change quality factors, like bass, treble, etc. If you're a musician who likes rendering their music clips on their computer, then you'll probably want to go with the more expensive option. Some brand names are Logitech, Alter Lansing, Sony, JBL, Kirsch, Creative Labs, Bose, and Harmon/Karson.

# 3C. - Protecting Your Investment

In *Back to the Future*, Doc gave Marty two potential outcomes about the risks of people interacting with their "future selves," the first indicating a face to face meeting might put the person into shock and two, it could create a "time paradox" causing a chain reaction in the space-time continuum, eventually destroying the entire universe!

While destroying the space time continuum is never a risk, viruses can be just as unpredictable as those two options. You might just get an annoying one that sticks adware all over your browser, or you can get one that's capable of destroying your entire operating system. They're unpredictable because people are coming up with new ones every single day. That's why it's not only important to have antivirus software, but you must keep it updated as it discovers new threats. It is not one of those software programs that when the "update available" dialog box pops up, you can just hit "remind me later". Instead, you need to go ahead and do that update as soon as possible.

How Viruses Spread – Usually the spread of a virus is not related to complex hacking of a system, but instead because people were not vigilant enough about their security. As I pointed out in the previous chapter, chain mail is a program designed to spread viruses, as are certain 'freewares' on the Internet. Failure to be vigilant about what you open and what you download will almost always be the cause of your computer getting infected.

That's why updated anti-virus software is a must. Not only will it keep people from gaining back door access to your computer, it will also scan anything you download to ensure it's not a known threat.

**Choosing a Security Software –** You can get your security software in one of two ways. You can buy the downloadable program for a onetime fee, or you can go with a subscription based service where you pay a monthly, or yearly renewal fee. How much you pay will be based on what the software provides.

**Anti-virus –** This software searches your hard drive for installed viruses and removes or quarantines them so they cannot infect the computer. These programs might cause excess folders or other programs to be installed, damaging your system and taking space on your hard drive.

**Anti-Spyware/Malware –** This is a software designed to stop running programs that are malicious from using your computer's resources. These programs might be tracking keystrokes or using your computer as a hub to send out spam or other problem emails.

**Firewall -** This is your computer's invisible wall that creates a one way route, where it allows you to send info out of your computer, while preventing unauthorized access into your computer.

**Antispam –** Anti-spam is mainly designed for email and diverts unsolicited advertisements to the spam folder, for quick and easy deleting. There is some form of it available on just about every place where you can receive messages, from instant messages to website comments.

**Browser based software –** Just about every browser comes with a built in software designed to block pop-up windows and prevent you from becoming a victim using it to search. Additional software can be downloaded to filter out inappropriate websites.

There are many good anti-virus/malware programs available. While Norton is a well-known and popular option, another one to consider is Security Suites, which gives a comprehensive listing of options designed to protect your computer.

However, all the best software in the world is no replacement for constant vigilance. That's why you need to remember these don'ts.

## Don'ts of Computer Use to Avoid Infection

- Don't open unsolicited attachments

- Don't download games or music from unfamiliar sites

- Don't open chainmail or anything with a suspicious subject line

- Don't ignore your computers' warning that a site may not be secure – If the browser is telling you it's not secure, it's usually not.

- Don't search out freeware. Freeware (copy programs that claim to give you expensive computer programs for free) are almost always viruses in disguise. A thorough Internet search of anything you're considering downloading will almost always tell you these are programs to avoid.

## 3D. - Understanding your operating system

Your computers' operating system is the platform that everything else relies on. That's why it's very important to use a software system designed to be compatible with the operating system. Macs are generally less virus prone than PCs, but a Mac can still pass on a PC based virus. See what your operating system recommends for virus protection in order to get the optimum results.

Here are some additional things to know about virus and malware protection.

The Editor's Choice Awards went to Norton Internet Security 2010 and 2011 as well as Norton 360 3.0. (This writer is a fan of Norton products, having tried at least two other manufacturers' over the years without satisfaction.) In 2016, in addition to Editor's Choices' of Symantec Norton Security Premium, Bitdefender Internet Security 2016, Bitdefender Total Security, Kaspersky Internet Security 2016, McAfee Live Safe 2016, Webroot, Comodo, and Trend Micro are also in the Top 10.

There are free security programs for those folks on an extremely tight budget. This author believes Internet Security is an investment well worth the annual cost. For more details about PC Mag's 2016 reviews, check out http://www.pcmag.com/article2/0,2817,2369749,00.asp

## 3E. - Social Engineering and Phishing

You may have heard of hacking in the past, and you may have used that term yourself. If your email got broken into or your bank account was compromised, you might have said "we've been hacked!"

And almost every person who says that is wrong. Hacker is a misappropriated term. In its early days, it was created at MIT as a way for engineers to find backways into systems. These engineers didn't always have malicious intent. Instead, hacking referred to the way they got to where they wanted to go, by taking advantage of certain loopholes in a system. Hackers used clever programming to gain unauthorized access to data.

Most of the time, when your information is compromised, you haven't been hacked as the person did not use programming to get your data. They used social engineering or phishing.

Social engineering, sometimes called Phishing, is a means of "human hacking." A person will pretend to be in a position of authority, or use fear in order to get you to give them sensitive account data that they can then use to get into your various accounts.

The most common method is those "PayPal Security Warning" emails you'll receive. If you have a PayPal account (or even if you don't) you'll receive a warning that your account has been compromised and you need to go to a certain webpage immediately and fill out the information in order to keep your account from being blocked.

These are almost always fraudulent. They might even look reputable and include company logos and professional language, but it should be noted that it's very easy to copy that kind of stuff. In addition, you can use an email spoofing program to make it look like anything you're sending is coming from a different address. Here's how you can avoid getting phished.

- If they contacted you via phone, do not give any information. Instead, tell them you're busy and you'll call them back. Verify nothing, not even your name and don't go to any website they tell you to. Just say you'll call them back. Then, call the number on the back of your bank card and ask to speak with someone in customer service. Above all DO NOT CALL THE NUMBER THEY GIVE YOU. Call the number for the financial institution as listed on your bankcard, or on their official website and discuss the issue with someone at your bank. Often, you'll find it was a phishing attempt.

- Do not follow links sent to you via email. Those links will usually lead to a spoofed site that looks like the real thing, but is only designed to capture your information.

- Look at the address bar. If you didn't follow rule number 2, you might notice the website you're at is slightly different, or has an additional number or two added. Another thing to note is if they have a secure box next to the address, like the below screenshot. No secure box usually equals spoofed site.

- Never underestimate scammers. They're coming up with new and clever ways to get your information all the time. Approach any unsolicited call or email with a heavy amount of suspicion and verify through your bank's official number.

- Report, report, report. PayPal wants all customers who receive these fraudulent emails to forward them so they can stop the scammers, as do most banks. When you get a spoofed email, send it on to your financial institution and hopefully save someone else from becoming a victim.

# 3F. - Common virus symptoms

While is often easy to know when you've been socially engineered or have your email compromised, it's a bit more difficult to figure out when your computer actually has been hacked. Here are a few warning signs.

- Your system is suddenly moving much slower than it used to. This is often a sign that a malicious piece of malware is using up your system's resources. Try this to check.

  - ◆ Press Ctrl+Alt+delete

  - ◆ Click on Task Manager

  - ◆ Search for any running programs that you don't recognize

  - ◆ Search these programs on the Internet to see if they're a threat. If so;

  - ◆ Run anti-malware to quarantine or remove these programs

  - ◆ *NOTE* - Keep in mind that there are a lot of things going on behind the scenes of your computer. Just because you don't recognize something does not mean it's a threat. It might just be a driver for another program. Don't shut the program down until you verify it actually is a threat

- There are suddenly icons on your toolbar you don't recognize, or your browser might have changed to one you've never used.

- Sudden crashing – While once might a fluke, if your computer is crashing regularly, that's almost always a sign of a virus.

- Certain disk drives are suddenly unusable. Maybe the CD rom won't work or you're getting a warning that you can't access a drive because you need admin privileges. If you own and set up the computer, you have admin privileges. If suddenly you don't, that could mean someone has changed those privileges to lock you out.

- File changes. If you have a lot more or a lot less files in your computer, but didn't download anything, chances are you have a virus.

- You're getting unusual error messages. An error message that is pure gibberish is often a sign of a virus.

Any time your computer shows one of these warning signs, do a virus search to locate and quarantine the virus. In addition, after this is done, change the password to your overall system and any accounts you might have accessed.

Staying safe on the Internet is about keeping your eye out for changes or risks, as well as being vigilant about what you allow to access your computer. Once your system is infected, it can be very hard to get rid of viruses. Your best bet to avoid expensive computer repairs is to enjoy the Internet with caution.

# CHAPTER 4
# A Journey into Open Cyberspace

## 4A. - Finding your way with Search Engines as your GPS

In the early 90s, search engines weren't hugely popular. Instead, the web was made up of portals, where you'd park your craft to get your email, see news headlines and find chatrooms all in the same spot. Companies made their money by banner advertising.

Then, Google got popular. See, Google offered an easy option for Internet users. They no longer had to be satisfied with what their portal delivered. Instead, they could find everything they needed with a simple search engine query. These days, Google has pretty much become synonymous with "search engine." Let's look at why.

### Google – The Closest thing to Artificial Intelligence

Google's biggest asset is their top secret algorithm. It's the behind the scenes coding that make any webpage you're looking for come up when you type certain keywords into the search bar. This algorithm used to be heavily focused on keywords, with the algorithm finding and returning sites with the highest count of these keywords.

Then came the spammers.

Spammers realized the best way to get one of those coveted spots in the first page of the search results, where 95% of website clicks go, was to simply do something called keyword stuffing. They'd create a paragraph of text and then stuff in a keyword that had absolutely nothing to do with it, simply in order to gain search traffic. Check out the example below using the keywords Louis Vuitton Discount Watches.

They were the most well-known LOUIS VUITTON DISCOUNT WATCHES kind of watch from their improvement in the sixteenth century until LOUIS VUITTON DISCOUNT WATCHES got to be mainstream after World War we amid which a transitional outline, LOUIS VUITTON DISCOUNT WATCHES, were utilized by the military. Pocket observes for the most part have a joined LOUIS

VUITTON DISCOUNT WATCHES chain to permit them to be secured to a waistcoat.

The above paragraph is pure gibberish. It doesn't tell us any kind of information about Louis Vuitton discount watches or even offer them for sale. Instead, it simply has a short paragraph that, in broken, jumbled English, kind of tells the history of watches in general.

The problem with the original Google algorithm was that it didn't understand context. Instead, it would simply match keywords and spit out the page with the most keywords. Spammers took full advantage and soon the search engine was filled with garbage sites.

So Google developed a new algorithm designed to think like a human. They had a test group of thousands of people, looking up keywords and rating the sites they found most relevant to those keywords. After they had the results, they used that to update their algorithm and search for context. In short, they created an algorithm that could think like a human being.

Many of the new search engines work this same exact way. Google is the most popular, taking about 80% of the market share in searches, so they set the standard when it comes to searches. But the goal of algorithms these days is to give the best organic search results that are the most relevant to a given query.

## 4B. - Organic and Paid Search – Knowing the difference

You may have heard the terms organic search versus paid search before and not been certain what they mean. Paid search isn't organized by algorithm, but instead by bid. The system set up is that business owners and ecommerce stores will create an ad. They will use that ad to target keywords relative to their industry. Then, they will pay a certain amount to get their business listed in the advertising area when a term is searched. These paid searches will appear in the advertising area on the search engines page, and usually you will see a discreet "Ad." Go ahead, try it: put "sound bars" (no quotes necessary) into Google search & there they are: https://www.google.com/?gws_rd=ssl#q=sound+bars

What's important to remember about paid search is that its *advertising focused*. It's like renting a billboard or paying for a newspaper ad. While it might get your item attention, the vast majority of people that understand the difference skip paid search in their search results in favor of organic search.

Organic search can't be paid for outright. It's determined by a number of factors that show a website is relevant in a given term or phrase.

You'll notice organic search results are geared toward *giving information*, with the assumption that someone searching for "paid search" isn't looking to buy a product, but instead wants to learn more about paid search. The Google algorithm knows from history that when people are searching for that term, that's usually what they want to see.

With organic search, you can't pay for your spot. You have to earn it. Google considers the content of the site, the status, websites linking into the site as a source as a way to determine that it's the most relevant for a given term. The more relevant a site is, the higher it goes up on the list. One of the biggest goals for business is to gain one of those top three spots for their chosen keywords.

That's because 62% of the clicks on search go to the top three results[11]. By the time you reach page two of the results, the entire page only gets around 5% overall. As a result, these high ranking search results are highly desirable for businesses.

# 4C. - Comprehending Cloud Storage

Cloud storage is in the Internet section, rather than peripherals, because it's completely virtual, making it exist in cyberspace, rather than as part of your computer. In the past, many businesses used cloud storage as a form of computer backup. The information they wanted to backup was safe at an offsite location, protecting their files in the event that their computer or even their network became damaged. However, due to newer advances in technology, it's now being used as a dynamic way to both save files and collaborate on them.

The major protection of cloud storage is in the way the data is distributed. Unlike in the days of physical storage, you aren't limited to a single location with a small amount of room. Instead, you can get as much room as you possibly need, as the storage is virtual and is ever expanding through more resources being added.

Of course, when you hear about cloud storage, you might think that it's something for big corporations, but in reality, there's a strong chance that you're already using cloud storage on a smaller scale. If you share documents through Google Drive or Dropbox, you're using cloud storage. If you have an iTunes account, chances are your music is being stored on the iCloud. Now, many of your items are being saved in a virtual place, making them accessible from anywhere and protecting you from the risk of data loss if your hard drive fails.

There's many great free options in cloud storage. If you're an Apple user, you'll be given immediate access to the iCloud, however, other storage options like OneDrive, Google Drive and Digital Dropbox are popular choices for people who want to store their items in a more secure cloud environment.

One thing to keep in mind is that you should still continue to store software and other necessary programs on your hard drive, as opposed to the cloud. Cloud storage is more for stationary items like documents, large files and backups. Programs that need to run constantly should be carried on your hard drive. For example, I save Word documents in a cloud storage file, but the software I need to run Word is saved on the hard drive.

**An Introduction to the Internet of Things –** The Internet of Things, or IoT, is gaining a lot of attention as our Internet experiences become less tied to our personal computers. These Internet connected devices are becoming part of our everyday lives, to the point where the Internet can help us do everything.

Much of this is because of leveraging the availability of cloud storage. Cloud storage is dynamic, so these smaller apps that companies want to run on all our connected items have a safe place to process, with the power they need. It is Cloud Storage that makes IoT possible. The future of IoT is pretty incredible. Here are a few things you can expect to see soon.

**"Click and collect" grocery delivery** – More and more major chains like Wal-Mart and Publix are trying out "Click and Collect' services, where customers install a grocery app on their phones and use it to pick and purchase the items they want. Then, they pay online and drive on over to the supermarket, where the groceries are bagged and waiting. This is a particularly important movement, as the grocery industry was one that once considered itself largely immune from the effects of the Internet.

**Micro-moments** – These are the moments that marketers will get you as you travel throughout your day with your iPhone or Apple Watch. You might suddenly get a notification as you walk past a Starbucks that you have a coupon or hear about a band you like holding a concert. Big data makes it possible for marketers to personalize messages, meaning that our devices might almost become omniscient when it comes to predicting our desires.

**Omni-channel experiences** – This is a new buzzword those in the retail industry are using to describe the merging of brick and mortar and internet shopping. These stores might add interactive displays and dynamic applications to storefronts to help merge Internet and brick and mortar customers into one base group.

**Self-Driving Cars** – More than a few companies are trying out self-driving cars with the hopes of making it the public transportation of the future. These cars use satellite navigation, and special sensors, in order to navigate roads efficiently. While these are still in their infancy, it's not unreasonable to expect to see self-driving cars go mainstream on the roads in our lifetime.

**Virtual Reality** – While this was rumored for years, Oculus Rift will be one of the first to actually make this happen. This highly anticipated gaming device is the first attempt to fully integrate people into the gaming experience and as this becomes more popular, it's likely that it will be incorporated into other areas, possibly causing it to go mainstream (like 3D did).

These are just a few advancements that Cloud Storage and the Internet have made possible. This additional power and capacity makes it possible to not just have the internet when we're using the computer, but instead carry it with us everywhere we go.

## 4D - Social Media and Networking

We can't talk about traveling the Internet without discussing social media sites. These are incredibly relevant in our society and can be used for everything from staying in touch with friends, to advertising, and business networking.

### Social Sites

Social sites are just what they sound like. They're primarily to let you contact family friends and even business associates. You can share photos and keep people updated to your status or even play games and find jobs. While there are many popular sites, and the use of such sites can change by region, here are some of the more popular social networking sites in the US.

**Facebook** – Facebook is the site that blew Myspace out of the water when it came to social networking. This site is by far the largest, with about 1.5 billion monthly active users[12]. The site is most popular to users ages 25 – 34, though other age groups enjoy it as well. It features profile and photo sharing options, as well as its own chat and video chat programs. Aside from having a friend page, if you're looking to gain recognition for a business or career pursuit, you can sign up for a fan page as well.

It's important to note that Facebook is a ripe breeding group for scams and hoaxes. In order to protect yourself, avoid accepting friend requests from people you don't know, and don't forward anything unless you check it on Snopes first. Also, while you can create groups for your friends and for your hobbies, and add your friends to them, it's considered bad form to add someone to a group without their permission.

Also, stop with the poking. Nobody likes pokes. They're just irritating. Ok, so that isn't much of a fact, but it is a request.

**Twitter –** Twitter is another popular choice, especially if you're a succinct kind of person. With Twitter, you're limited to 140 characters (including spaces) but you can also post links, short videos and more. Twitter has about 140 million users who send about 340 million tweets per day[13].

Communication is done via direct messages with the @ sign or categorized subject via the # sign. Twitter is most popular under the youngest adult demographic, ages 18-29, with 87% of that age group having an account[14].

**LinkedIn –** LinkedIn is a site designed for business professionals that want to network in the business world. As a result, it's a more formal site where your posts and updates should be focused on how you'd behave in a professional environment. The profile there is mainly based on work and educational experience. It's also

a good place to meet up with former business contacts and even search for new opportunities.

LinkedIn has nearly 330 million users[15], with just over one third of those users being in the United States. Amazingly, one in three professionals use LinkedIn today. If you're looking for new opportunities in business, or seeking out a new job, then you should know that it's very likely that any company you apply with is going to look for a LinkedIn account. Having a complete, professional profile is the best choice.

## Photo and Media Sites

Photo and media sites are a bit more streamlined than social sites, in that the items on them are media based and not text based. Many can be viewed without joining, though if you want to upload, you'll need to set up an account. Here are some of the more popular photo and Media sites

**YouTube –** YouTube is primarily a video sharing site, though if you want to place a video elsewhere, you can also use it as a video hosting site. YouTube has over a billion users[16], both uploading and watching videos every day. Another great choice is Vimeo.

**Pinterest –** Pinterest is another hugely popular site, though most of the posting is done by boards, in that people will pin items onto a board for reviewing such as a small group of photos.

**Hulu/Netflix –** I've put these two together as they are so much more than simple media streaming sites. These are paid subscription sites that many people are using as cable replacement services. Not only can these sites be viewed on laptop and desktop computers, items like Roku's and gaming systems allow users to stream these videos right to their TV, ending the need for expensive cable plans.

## Mostly Mobile Sites

Some sites are really better used as smartphone apps. Mostly, these sites are focused on photo sharing, so they've become more popular for Android and iOS use.

**Instagram –** Instagram is a photo sharing site that mainly features users uploading pictures, along with hashtags in order to categorize those pictures. Instagram is another hugely popular platform, with 400 million monthly users[17]

**Snapchat –** Snapchat is a unique site that features something special called ephemeral messaging. As explained in an earlier chapter, ephemeral messaging is messaging that deletes itself so you won't have to worry about those naughty pics coming back to haunt you.

## Blogging Sites

Blogging sites are great if you're a writer or artist who wants to share their work online. With them you can create a running blog with your stories, poetry and photos in order to grow a fan base or just share your thoughts. Many of these sites are also free, allowing you to create a professional looking website without having to pay much, or anything at all. Here are some good choices.

Note which one is not "secured." The "s" after http stands for TLS = Transport Layer Security (or formerly SSL = Secure Sockets Layer.) This is used by website intent on confidentiality.

- https://blogger.com

- http://www.wix.com

- https:/weebly.com

- https://Wordpress.com

A note on WordPress – When going to wordpress.com, remember the .com. WordPress also has a self-hosted platform that requires you to have a server and host your own site. This can be draining on your computer and expensive. Wordpress.com, on the other hand, is platform hosted, meaning that you won't have to worry about servers. Personally, I prefer the professionalism of a site reflecting my name, or business name, or product name but this is your choice.

## Online dating sites

One final platform of social sites you might run into are online dating sites. While Match.com and PlentyofFish.com have been popular low cost options over the years, other dating apps like Grindr and Tinder allow users to browse singles in their area and meet people. As these new sites pop up every single day, the list is constantly being updated. Of course, these types of sites also feature online fakers and predators, otherwise known as Catfish.

# 4E. - Finding Online Easter Eggs

While you might think of those old Egg Hunts when you were a kid, online Easter Eggs are actually available any time of year. Easter Eggs are nothing more than neat lines of code that users can interact with. They might take you to a hidden webpage, or they might turn your search into an Atari game. There are millions of hidden nooks on the internet to explore and probably the most famous for their online Easter Eggs is Google.

## Google's Easter Eggs

Google is always adding and updating its famous search engine, and the people who maintain it have a sense of humor. There's more than a few neat things you can do with Google, and while some are temporary, some have been around for years. While this list includes some particularly fun ones, it's by no means comprehensive, as Google is always developing new Easter Eggs.

**Askew –** Searching askew will tilt your screen slightly.

**Atari Breakout -** Want to get retro and play some Atari breakout? Simply search Atari Breakout in Google Images and your image homepage will turn into an interactive version of Super Breakout!

**Bacon number –** sick of losing at Six Degrees of Kevin Bacon? Type any actor's name+ Bacon Number and Google will reveal their degrees of separation, as well as exactly how the actors are related.

**Bletchley Park –** This is one of those 'you had to be there' jokes. Searching Bletchley Park results in the Google places account coming up as though it's being decoded. Bletchley Park is the location of the U.K.'s code-breaking center, which helped the allies break axis power codes in WWII

**Blink HTML –** Here's one for coders. Searching the phrase "Blink HTML" will make all instances of the word blink…blink.

**Conway's game of life –** Typing this in will result in a life simulation blob appearing on the right hand side of the screen. It's probably one of the more boring of the Easter Eggs.

**Do a barrel roll –** searching that phrase in Google will, you guessed it, make your screen do a barrel roll.

**Festivus –** Searching Festivus adds a Festivus pole to the side of your screen, though during non-holiday seasons, it will just be a pole.

**Flip a Coin –** Typing flip a coin will start an animation of a coin flip, with a random head or tail result.

**Fun Facts –** Searching fun facts will result in a random piece of trivia popping up.

**Google in 1998 –** Typing Google in 1998 will result in your screen reverting to Google copying Yahoo!'s 1998 layout.

**Google Pacman –** This gives you a Pacman game to play right on the search screen.

**Roll a die –** Similar to flip a coin, roll a die will give you a random six sided dice roll result.

**Zerg rush –** This turns your search screen into another game, as Os will begin to devour your search results if you don't fight them off by clicking!

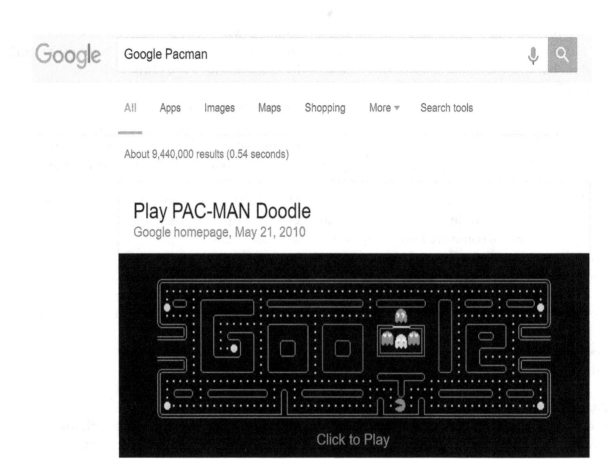

Play PAC-MAN Doodle
Google homepage, May 21, 2010

Click to Play

PAC-MAN™ & ©1980 NAMCO BANDAI Games Inc.

## Other Easter Egg Websites

There are thousands of sites that use Easter Eggs, but no one has found all of them. Here are a few that are known as well as how to find the Easter Egg on the site.

**British Vogue –** at http://www.vogue.co.uk/, if you type in up arrow + up arrow + down arrow + down arrow + left + right + left + right + B + A while on the home page, a dinosaur in a hat will run across the bottom of your screen!

**BuzzFeed –** Using up arrow + up arrow + down arrow + down arrow + left + right + left + right + B + A on the Buzzfeed main page will reset it to a theme. In the past, it was clothes, but it updates frequently.

**Digg –** If you enter up arrow + up arrow + down arrow + down arrow + left + right + left + right + B + A at Digg.com, you'll get Rickrolled, aka you'll get a surprise video of the 1987 Rick Astley song "Never Gonna Give You Up."

**Hema –** This Dutch retailer has a unique set up when you go to this page; http://producten.hema.nl/ This one is amazing! All you have to do is nudge the blue cup with your mouse, and then watch what happens.

**Wikipedia –** Search Easter Egg on Wikipedia, and it will come back with its own Easter egg. Simply hover on hedgehog in the picture.

When the hedgehog is clicked on, it goes to a basket of Easter Eggs.

I'm a hedgehog, not an egg!

This image reveals a hidden "Easter egg" when the mouse pointer is hovered over the hedgehog at the bottom right.[1]

## Testing Things Out

There's a ton of different ways to find Easter eggs on sites, but most of it is luck and guess-work. It doesn't hurt to click around a new or interesting page to see what will happen with it.

In addition, a lot of sites use the Konami Code, so try entering it when you're on a new page. This is a code that found its origins in video games and is used so frequently, it's kind of considered an industry cheat code. It's the same one given for British Vogue and Digg. Again, it's;

*up arrow + up arrow + down arrow + down arrow + left + right + left + right + B + A*

On top of the Konomi code, often, you'll find things via hidden link. Finding hidden links on a website has its share of guess work, but its most easily done by viewing the source code. Viewing the source code is as easy as right clicking on any webpage to pull up the 'inspect' option;

Once you click on Inspect, you see a side (or lower screen) open that reveals some of the coding for the page, as shown in this image.

This is a place where you can often find an anomaly or two. See if there's a hidden message, or link that isn't obvious. While some links are simply image files, others might be hidden pages!

Don't be afraid to experiment with the sites you're on to see if you can find a secret trick.

## 4F. Social Media's Dirty Little Secrets

While most of the Internet's illicit activities can be found on the Darknet, there's more than a few that are happening right in plain view. From drug deals going down on Instagram, to gun sales on EBay, every social media site has a group using it for illicit purposes.

Now, before we get started, it should probably be noted that every one of these social media sites makes a concentrated effort to stop such activities, and site policies prohibit them, but the problem is so widespread, no one site could monitor and stop it all.

**EBay's Illegal Auctions –** Here's a unique way some people get around gun laws. They buy gun parts on EBay and put the weapon together themselves. For example, if you were to try to buy an AR 15 assault rifle, you couldn't do it on the site, but you could buy every single piece for it, with the exception of the lower receiver that can be purchased by a second hand seller. Simply searching AR 15 results in over 100 results, though simply searching for a specific part will often do the trick.

Instagram Drug Dealers – While you can find both real and fake drug dealers on the Internet, recent trends have them working on Instagram, using hashtags for marketing. Simply typing in a slang term for marijuana or other drugs, along with the area where the person is looking can help users find marijuana dealers online. It's pretty simple to do:

Number 1 – Type in the area plus the drug.

*For example: #orlandoweed*

*Step 2 – Click on one of the results.*

*Step 3 – Locate the dealer's contact info by clicking on the posters name, as in image below with circle and horizontal line, top right.*

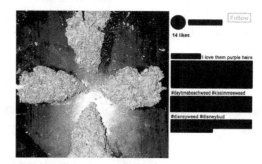

The dealer will usually request in their contact info that someone direct message (DM) them on Instagram, or add them on a messaging site like kik. Once that's done, the dealer and the buyer will make payment arrangements or arrange to meet in person. While this is a simpler approach to online drug buying, it's also highly risky and the honeypot sting, where Law Enforcement pretends to be a dealer to get buyers, is common.

Again, this is a practice that Instagram works to fight, but as the dealers come up with new acronyms and hashtags every day to advertise wares, it can be very difficult to stop. This practice is similar on Twitter though Instagram is more popular due to the photo-centric nature of the site.

**Terrorism on Twitter and YouTube -** ISIS and other terrorist organizations are known for using social media sites like Twitter and YouTube for propaganda videos and recruiting young extremists. So far, Twitter has suspended at least 1000 accounts with suspected ties to terrorism. While YouTube has taken down countless videos, more are added every day. Organizations like Isis and Al-Qaida use many different social media sites, but YouTube and Twitter stand out because of their early 20s demographic. Terrorists have been posting propaganda videos aimed at people in this age group in order to gather new recruits. So far, about 5000 westerners have left their homes to join terrorist organizations and many were recruited by social media. Both Twitter and YouTube are mainly dependent on users flagging in order to ban these accounts and remove propaganda content.

## 4G - Naughty Niche Sites

Aside from these dark sides of normal social media, there are many niche sites out there that are designed specifically for illegal, elicit or unethical groups. These sites can be broken down to a few different types based on their goal.

**Hate Sites –** Hate sites can often fall into shock site category as well, as they're run for the purpose of putting down one group simply to gain attention and viral status. These hate sites also include bullying sites and revenge porn sites. Some examples of such sites include;

- **Burnbook –** Burnbook is an app that's gaining popularity with teens. While most sites seem to be anti-bullying, Burnbook was designed *for* bullying. Burnbook is named after the controversial book kept in the movie "Mean Girls" and allows users to post anonymously, without signing in, about any user. The whole purpose is to pick a name, or a subject, and pass judgment on it. Because it's anonymous, it's a breeding ground for bullying.

- **TheDirty.com –** This site is a revenge content site that may include naked pics of exes, or simply personal information people would not want shared. This is a site dedicated to doxing and covers celebrities as well.

- **MyEx.com –** A site where 'revenge porn' is popular, in that users will submit naked pictures of their exes and give out personal information. Several states are passing measures to make 'revenge porn' a crime, but not all states have anything in place.

- **Return of the Kings –** This is an anti-feminist website that offers articles and community links supporting alpha-male behavior, and has been accused of endorsing rape and violence against women. Common article titles include "German Government Cuckholds Its Men By Teaching Migrants How To Sleep With German Women" and "5 More Reasons I No Longer Date Black Women."

Shock Sites – These sites typically feature content designed to be shocking, disgusting or offensive. The goal of these sites is to gain viral views. Some examples of shock sites include;

- **Two Girls One Cup –** This viral, obscene and literally vomit inducing video was set up on its own home site, and spurred such a strong reaction there are thousands of reaction videos on YouTube of people watching the infamous short.

- **Tub Girl –** Another upsetting image that's just plain unwatchable. These shock sites frequently feature innocuous names, hiding seriously awful images. They're created with the hopes of gaining viral hits by any means necessary.

**Violence Porn –** These sites are sites for all those people who slow down to look at the car crash on the side of the road. Autopsy photos, accident photos, gruesome wounds and serious injuries can all be found for the violence enthusiasts out there.

- **Murderpedia.org –** An encyclopedia of murders, murderers and more, this site is frequently known to feature crime scene photos.

- **Rotten Dot Com –** One of the original violence porn sites, Rotten.com has been in business since 1996, featuring mostly pictures of murder and violence victims, with a few car crashes thrown in.

**Lifestyle/Political Sites –** Free Market/Political sites are those sites that people put up which might break laws both moral and actual. These sites might embrace or encourage alternative or sometimes dangerous lifestyles. Some examples include;

- **Anonhq.com -** The official website of hacktivist group anonymous.

- **LiveLeak –** LiveLeak is a website made of user generated content. It initially gained infamy in 2007 after the execution of Saddam Hussein was illegally posted, and more recently, was one of the sites showing the beheading of James Foley. The site often features graphic videos of violence in foreign and conflict- ridden countries.

- **Lost All Hope –** This is a site that offers advice and tips for those considering suicide, from an unbiased perspective, meaning it's less about preventing suicide, and more about teaching others to commit it painlessly. Similar sites have been shut down for offering this advice.

- **The Pirate Bay –** This site features both legal and illegal torrent downloads for finding TV shows, movies and music files.

- **PUA forums –** This is a community specifically for pick up artists and people sharing tips on manipulating the opposite sex.

- **The Pro-Ana Lifestyle Forever –** This is a site dedicated to pro-ana, or pro-anorexia, where anorexics view the disease not as a problem, but a lifestyle choice. The site offers tips and support for anorexics.

- **We Be High –** A site dedicated to reviewing marijuana strains, finding marijuana and marijuana tourism.

Just about anything has a site, and a social media presence dedicated to it. Whether its legal or illegal, moral or immoral, or sometimes just plain disgusting, if you can type it into Google, you can find it online. After all, the Internet mirrors the real world, and in reality, we are a very strange people.

# 4H. - All About Catfishing

If you've seen MTVs Catfish, then you'll understand the term. If not, a Catfish is a person who pretends to be someone else online. The term Catfish was coined after a man named Nev Schulman started talking to a pretty young woman online. The two developed a very close relationship, but the girl would not agree to meet up with him or do any kind of video chat.

But Nev Schulman was a documentary filmmaker and a pretty good investigator. He decided to go on a road trip, to investigate this girl. When he finally arrived at her door, it turned out that the beautiful young cellist he thought he'd been talking to was actually a much older woman.

Nev was depressed, until his friend pointed out that catfish are frequently added to cod tanks in order to keep the cod active. It was a metaphor for what had happened to Nev, because despite the fact that the girl wasn't real, she'd made him active. She'd made him social and she'd made him take a step that changed his life. In short, he was the cod. She was the catfish.

And the term Catfish was born.

People who pretend to be other people online are known as Catfish and they have a wide range of reasons for doing it. They might simply be lonely, or it could be for more nefarious reasons. The risks of this are high, as anyone can claim to be anyone behind an anonymous computer screen.

To avoid getting taken in by one of these scams, here are some things you should be aware of;

- People with very few photos, or very few friends on their profile are often not who they say they are.

- Anyone who claims to be an American person living overseas in some high profile job should be taken with a grain of salt. Especially note if they're coming from places that have a high amount of Internet scams, like the Ukraine, Nigeria or the Philippines, to name a few.

- If they won't video chat or send updated photos, chances are they have something to hide.

- When in doubt, verify their images. That's easy with a simple Google image search.

  1. Simply go to an image on the profile, right click and select "copy image URL".

  2. Go to Google Images.

  3. Click on the camera.

4. Copy in the link. If the image shows up under multiple websites, chances are you're being duped.

Above all, never send money to anyone and don't get invested in a relationship if the person you're talking to refuses something as simple as a video chat. It's the easy way to avoid getting sucked into a Catfish scheme.

# 41. Internet auctions and payment gateway services

Want to buy your own DeLorean or a pair of self-lacing sneakers? Luckily for you, places like eBay have all that and more available. Heck, simply searching the phrase "Time Machine" gives me 12,900 results!

EBay's an auction shop that is very well known. In fact, it's the number one online auction site. However, there are others out there including;

- **uBid:** http://www.ubid.com

- **WebStore:** http://www.webstore.com

- **eBid:** http://www.ebid.net

- **eBid US:** http://us.ebid.net

- **bid4assets (real estate+):** http://www.bid4assets.com

- **Bidz (jewelry):** http://www.bidz.com

- **Online Auction:** http://www.onlineauction.com

- **WeBidz:** http://www.webidz.com

These are some of the more popular sales sites that offer auction bidding in order for you to get the best bang for your buck. http://www.Internetauctionlist.com/ is a good place to go in order to get a comprehensive listing of online actions as well.

Most of these sites will allow you to auction off your items for free, or a nominal fee. In addition, if you're interested in selling things outright, Etsy and Shopify are great sites for setting up your own storefront to sell just about anything you can think of.

In addition, payment apps are becoming a popular choice in paying for your items or sending money quickly and easily. PayPal is one such site you can use, while there are other good ones as well;

- **Google Checkout:** https://checkout.google.com

- **Intuit Go Payment:** http://payments.intuit.com

- **Authorize:** http://www.authorize.net

Payment gateways allow you to send payments without having to share your credit or debit card information. In addition, these sites often have easy dispute methods in place for blocking users from taking unauthorized funds without proof. Now that you have both the basics and the intermediate level stuff down, let's move on into more advanced topics, with everything from ZIP files and protecting your privacy with VPNs, to delving into the offerings of the deep web. Before moving on and exploring these areas, it's best to make sure that you've been doing the responsible thing and updating that anti-virus software as necessary.

# SECTION 3 – ADVANCED FLIGHT ON THE RAGGEDY EDGE

*Humanity has advanced, when it has advanced, not because it has been sober, responsible, and cautious, but because it has been playful, rebellious, and immature.*

- Tom Robbins, American Author

http://www.brainyquote.com/search_results.html?q=advanced+flight

# CHAPTER 5
# Optional Tools For The Journey

There are various online tools out there that you can use to make your Internet experience easier. Some you'll find that you'll need to use eventually, while others you may never have to worry about. In this section I'm going to discuss a few of these optional tools and how you can use them to your advantage.

## 5A. - Understanding ZIP Utilities

If you need to send a large file or document, then often compressing that file will make it easier to send. To do this, you'll want to use a ZIP utility. Most likely, you already have one installed on your computer. These programs will allow you to compress the file for easy sending.

So when exactly do you need a ZIP utility? Consider a case where you're working on a large project and you have all your documents in a file folder. That file folder contains 30 documents. If you try to simply attach it to your email, it won't let you attach the folder. Instead, you'll need to send those documents separately. Sometimes, your email won't let you do this. In addition, it's kind of a pain in the backside. So instead, you zip those files together and send them all as one.

This is incredibly easy to do. I have a file folder that I need to send to a colleague's editor. It contains at least ten documents and her editor would gladly murder her if I just attached all ten to the email. So I'm going to zip it into a new folder for sending.

Step #1 – I'll right click on the file folder that I want to zip.

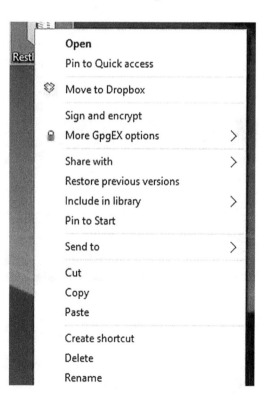

Step #2 - Then, I'm going to go to the "Send to" menu" and select "send to" and then, "compressed (zipped) folder".

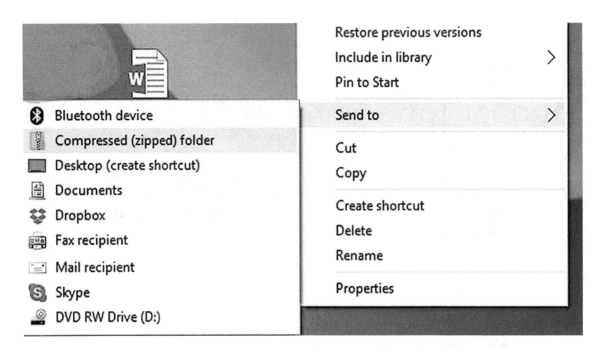

Step #3 – Now, you'll see the new zipped file is next to the old one. The zipped one is obviously the one with the zipper.

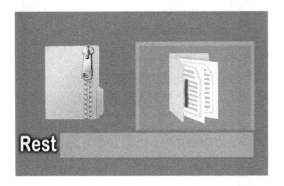

Now, I can send that zipped file just how I'd send any other document.

You'll be able to tell if you have a zip utility installed simply in that right click. If sending to

compressed file is an option, then you have one preinstalled. If not, there are several programs you can download that are relatively low cost.

**WinZip:**
http://www.winzip.com/win/en/index.htm

**7-Zip:** http://www.7zip.com

**PK Zip:**
http://www.pkware.com/software/pkzip/

One thing I need to bring up in this section is that often, when you do need to send a large amount of files, rather than going with a zip utility, using cloud storage is an equally feasible, and often better option. With cloud storage, only one document that everyone can work on is available at all times. With the ZIP utility, you need to keep sending documents back and forth as you edit them. ZIP is quickly becoming obsolete for some users due to this.

Of course, giving someone access to your shared document also means that they might be able to make changes to that document. If that makes you uncomfortable, then sharing large files is still best done through zip.

# 5B. - PGP or Pretty Good Privacy

If you don't send a lot of top secret info, chances are you don't know a lot about PGP and GNU. PGP stands for "Pretty Good Privacy". This is a coding system that was developed by Symantec in order to send private, encrypted messages. When hearing about it these days, it's become synonymous with GNU Privacy Guard

Mainly, this software works by changing plain, readable text into cypher text. This is all managed through a secret key that is used to both conceal and reveal the text. If you've ever seen something like this:

-----BEGIN PGP PUBLIC KEY BLOCK-----

Version: PGP Universal 2.9.1 (Build 347)

MQMuBFG3x4URCACZ/c7PjmPwOy2qIyKAYRftIT7YurxmZ/wQEwkyLJ4R+A2mFAvw

EfdVjghAKwnXxqeZO9WyAEofqIX5ewXD9J4H6THaWNlDeNwnIUhbVsSEgT6iwGEG

arXvkrMyy+U5KA0x2dcsYRKAPMM1db+4zSQkWTWzufLU7lcKi3gU3pNTxSA0DjCn

wfJQspiyWchSfgZ59+fKaGZJVSElrS2i2ok5mK3ywCXRWvnAC/VxA3N6T4jvkX/+

1gS/oUgdocP31TeV0L20JH9QgmFYC3jMbErAATo2x9Y8g4NofdvSnntbZk9Giycc

cgOWsa8aFtTjvcBp8hkCl3dK5xTZiY0gLSaDAQCXSHI7zw4LiNFfCV+PbO9BEqDA

i4JFV/qX7TgfBNX7nwf/fEFu18V16lVCsRzeuhMsHHzAQ7PZJfdfhyOubq0fnjkk

2RdcleosnP22zP5LoRs1fvIDdL3wnkg1ZUwfICP0HWRzRYcVBaIv9HcqSVBWriJj

uscni5QtX3fIU2wqSyP90wquWPkO7jObT0hWihhWPFXiFA6996i/rTZiJH+eFPSW

afxVlRAqH4kaUBen5fSMbBSsfc+GkuuQH7gIYQC2k88soPLuFZGsibDwBqvdUqFG

S39ifNf/2MUx8DrM8bbIPPwiuTelAFVPu7GGzyzAF3yhk/Cdd/YmWlwrwAd4Psev

then you've already been exposed to PGP. If you want to exchange encrypted messages with someone, then they will need access to your PGP key in order to decipher them. The biggest use for this is in email. There are many PGP clients that can be added to a basic emailing program, in order to conceal the body text. Just keep in mind that when using PGP for email, the body text will be encrypted, while the heading and to/from email text won't.

Another common use for PGP is creating verifiable Internet signatures. The program uses your private key info with the document you want to sign to create a digital signature that is verifiably yours, meaning other online individuals can't forge your digital signature.

While there are many good options of encrypting items, the two best options are Gpg4win (http://www.gpg4win.org/index.html) for Windows users and GPG Suite for Mac (https://gpgtools.org/).

Specifically leaning how to use this encryption can take a while. It would actually be an entire book in and of itself. It's easier to figure it out by watching it done in video, so here are three links to the tutorial videos I used when I first started using this program.

- **Installation –** https://youtu.be/ZMfFGkYibNQ

- **Generating Keys –** https://youtu.be/NDGpQlAU4PM

- **Encrypting and Decrypting –** https://youtu.be/Cbv4jPIJ8J8

On the upside, the need to use this type of encryption is relatively rare. You'll only run into it when sending sensitive email, creating verified signatures, or if you're about to do something bad on the Darknet.

# 5C. - Virtual Private Networks (or VPNs)

VPNs, otherwise knowns as virtual private networks are a useful tool in hiding your computers IP address. They are created by networking together a bunch of computers, running over various countries, making your IP completely anonymous, or even making it look like you're coming from another country.

The VPN requires that you log in via a 'client' which is pretty much just a start screen. Once in, all of the data you send and receive on the Internet is private, meaning outside hackers can't see it.

## When to use a VPN

One of the best times to use a VPN is when you're working from an Internet hot spot. Free Wi-Fi that businesses use is often rife with scammers who want to use the data your computer takes in to slip inside your system and gain access to your credentials. Making your computer secure through the use of the VPN makes it less of a target to hackers and much harder to infiltrate.

Another time is when you use a program like BitTorrent to download items. Often, companies will use IP addresses to hunt down your email to send things like cease and desist letters, believing that just having the software installed is a sign that you're pirating their stuff. It's a common scare tactic to do this, and simply having a BitTorrent program installed is not illegal. To stay off of these witch hunt lists, a VPN makes you harder to find.

Finally, if you regularly obtain sensitive information over a computer network, like at a school or a business, chances are your organization already has their own VPN in place.

Anyone who is concerned about their privacy would do well to get a VPN. You don't have to use them all the time, but they are useful if you're traveling and need to use a hotspot, or if you have sensitive info on your computer that you don't want people to find.

## Where to get a VPN

Keep in mind that not all VPN services are created equally. They are only as strong as their network and some have terrible networks. When considering that, here are a few that most users find to be secure.

- **Private Internet Access -** https://www.privateInternetaccess.com/

- **ProXPN -** https://www.proxpn.com/index.php

- **TorVPN -** torvpn.com/information.html

- **TorGuard -** http://torguard.net/

- **WiTopia -** https://www.witopia.net/

That brings us to the end of the more advanced tools you can use on the Internet. Well, the regular Internet anyway. In the next chapter, we're going to delve into the mysteries of the deepweb, the Internet's oldest and largest resource.

# CHAPTER 6
# Delving into the Deep Web

## 6A. – Deep Web v. Darknet

You might have heard the deep web referred to as the Darknet. It should be noted that these two terms aren't technically the same. The deep web is simply the unsearchable part of the Internet, while the Darknet is where illegal activities occur in the areas. For the purpose of simplicity, we're going to use the term deep web when going over this chapter, regardless of what area we're discussing.

This is a place that Marty McFly could never have dreamed of. It is the raggedy edge of cyberspace and for brave travelers only. There's a lot to explore, because it's estimated to be 500x[18] bigger than the surface Internet.

## 6B. – The history of the deep web

If you've never heard of it, that's not surprising. See, the deep web was part of the original Internet, but it was a more confusing, less organized place. But during the 1980s, better networking protocols were created and the deep web just became a dumping ground for old government papers. The deep web didn't really begin to boom again until the late 1990s.

By then, the Internet was booming and while most people stuck to mainstream sites, those who wanted to get their hands on copyrighted material would take to the deep web to find that material and download it.

Then, in March of 2000 Ian Clarke released Freenet[19], a revolutionary program that allowed one to reach into the deep web part of the web with virtually no likelihood of being tracked. The deep web became more nefarious than simple illegal downloads. Instead, it became a place that ran on crime. Over time, more and more developers came up with unique software until the deep web was rife with hidden, impossible to find sites.

Today, the Deep web is home to all forms of questionable activities. Everyone from extremist groups, to personal liberty groups, to criminals looking to make a buck, use the deep web to engage in business and communicate with others in their organization. While the NSA has been unable to explore the network itself to find these individuals, there have been some rumors that they've been able to exploit vulnerabilities in existing user software to find out who they are.

But based on the size, the complexity and how it works, the deep web will probably always be the most anonymous place you can be online.

## 6C. - How to get to the Deep Web

One thing to note is it's impossible to get to the deep web from a regular Browser like Internet Explorer or Firefox. You must have a special browser installed in order to be able to use it. You'll need a deep web browser instead. The most popular deep web browser is Tor, otherwise known as the Onion Router. The browser is available for free download.

Tor - https://www.torproject.org/

The Onion Router might seem like a strange name - that is until you look at the extensions. While most regular websites end in a .com, or an .org, or a .gov and so on, all Tor links end in an .onion.

## 6D. - How it's anonymous

There are many ways that Tor stays anonymous. The first is in the way it's designed. Much like a VPN, the TOR network bounces off of a network of volunteer computers. This allows people to browse without websites being able to track the location, because everything on Tor is constantly moving.

It's hard to hit a moving target.

The next thing that makes Tor anonymous is how it's organized. In short, it's not. Tor doesn't have a search engine. There's no algorithm picking things out for you. You can't even tell where you're going by the URL. Here are a few random Tor URLs.

- http://3g2upl4pq6kufc4m.onion/

- http://xmh57jrzrnw6insl.onion/

- http://zqktlwi4fecvo6ri.onion/

There is no way to know what those URLs lead to by looking at them and every URL on the network looks like that. As a result, there are many hidden search pages within the Tor network where you can go to find listings and search pages. Those three links above are actually Tor search pages within the network.

None of those search pages are very comprehensive. It's impossible for there to be an entire listing of links and where they go. Instead, most of them will include a limited number of links and where they go.

This is all by design. While the goal of most sites on the surface web are to be found, the goal of most sites on the deep web are to never be found (to avoid detection by authorities). As a result, to use Tor, you need to know where you're going already, to find a way to get there.

*It truly is that universal paradox that Doc was talking about.*

# 6E. - What's There To Do On The Deep Web?

The short answer to that question is probably nothing you should be doing. I've always compared the deep web to the regular Internet like this:

The regular Internet is like walking through a park in suburban Connecticut on a sunny summer day. While bad things can happen, they're pretty unlikely. The deep web is like wandering around Chicago's South Side at midnight on New Year's Eve. It's only a matter of time before you run into something bad.

Sites like the Silk Road (now shut down by the FBI) and the Agora Marketplace are pretty much the Amazon of the Black Market. Drugs, fraudulent credit cards, hackers and more are available through payment of a digital currency known as Bitcoin. On top of that, it's also a hub for terrorist chatrooms (yeah, they have those) child pornography and even hitmen for hire.

But the deep web also has its good uses. In countries where having an opinion is a crime, bloggers and activists use it to get to sites and post information without facing repercussions. Activists also use it in order to set up secret meetings without having to worry about public disclosure. Just think of it. Somewhere on the deep web, Anonymous is having a meeting on how to bring down Isis as you're reading this.

It's the utmost in privacy protection. Sites can't track you and people can't find you (for the most part) when you use it.

# 6F. - Darknet Shopping

When it comes to buying illegal items on the Darknet, and on the web in general, there's a lot of skepticism. You can't really blame the skeptics. After all, if the drug dealer you send money to on the Internet bails with your cash, exactly what is your recourse? You can't sue them or file a complaint with the ISP. You're certainly not going to call the cops. So of course, many look at this and say, 'there's no way that this online drug dealer is legit."

And the Darknet, as well as a few social media sites, found a way to work around that. On the Darknet, using the right platform, it's completely possible to vet any vendor in order to avoid most scams. This begins with choosing the right marketplace.

## Intro to Darknet Marketplaces
Scam marketplaces probably cost the most money to Darknet buyers. Sometimes, the scams are intentional from the beginning. Sometimes, they're scams of opportunity. Most often, they're something called "exit scams."

Setting up a website for vendors requires a lot of work. On the Darknet, you can't just install a shopping cart based website and make it work. Instead, you need to write the code for your website, ensure it's extremely secure, discreetly find vendors, help those vendors find customers and above all, manage all the financial transactions.

And while the site owner is doing all of this, they're also trying as hard as possible to be completely anonymous. After all, what they're doing is a big deal. They all remember the Dread Pirate Roberts.

The Dread Pirate Roberts was a man named Ross William Ulbricht who ran one of the biggest Darknet market sites, Silk Road. His arrest in October of 2013 gave the Darknet worldwide attention. Ulbricht was charged with everything from drug trafficking to money laundering and attempted murder. He was later sentenced to life in prison without parole.

So these site owners are taking a big risk, and the most common case of exit scams result because of fear. An individual will set up a market, start getting a lot of traffic to that market, and panic. Because they worked so hard to conceal their identity, they can then shut down the site and take all the bitcoins in the site's accounts with them.

To avoid winding up on one of these sites, it's important to ensure that the sites are established and are consistently adding new features to improve ease of use. DeepDotWeb is probably the most comprehensive place to look at the statistics of any market. Users can browse this, and other sites like Reddit, to see user comments on any marketplace or vendor. Some of the warning signs of a coming exit scam in a marketplace include

- Lots of users complaining that the site is moving incredibly slow (this could be a DDOS attack or simply the owner scaling down)

- Lots of users complaining that Bitcoin is missing from their accounts, or Bitcoins never showed up after sending them

- Complaints of non-responsive webmasters when starting a dispute

- Vendors announcing they're leaving that particular market without giving a reason. (This is sometimes because the vendor is given advance warning of the upcoming exit scam)

- It's a brand new market, filled with outrageously low prices

- Users complain that withdrawals from their accounts are blocked

The best place to see what users are saying about various Darknet sites is at https://www.reddit.com/r/darknet. Before someone deposits any money to a Darknet account, that site should be vetted thoroughly. The marketplace itself often has a lot of responsibility over a large amount of cash. That teamed with the fear of getting caught makes exit scamming very tempting. Choosing the right marketplace is the first step to avoiding scams on Darknet vendor sites.

## Understanding the Escrow System

The very thing that keeps individuals from getting scammed by vendors is often the same thing that gets vendors taken for millions: the escrow system. The escrow system allows these sites to operate at all, because it allows a certain level of protection to people considering making a purchase. Here's how it works:

1. The shopper deposits money from their bitcoin wallet, to their own individual bitcoin address set up on the market site. The deposit address will usually be in the account information and will be updated regularly, so the user will deposit to a new address every single time to improve security. Most sites auto-update bitcoin deposit addresses.

2. The shopper chooses a vendor and makes a purchase.

3. Once the purchase is confirmed, the money is deposited into an administrative escrow wallet, which neither the buyer, nor the vendor has access to.

4. The buyer receives their product and 'finalizes' the sale, authorizing the site admin to transfer the money from escrow, to the vendor. Or, the buyer does not receive their product and files a dispute, freezing the escrow funds during the dispute process.

These are not the drug dealers of the past. Vendors at the Darknet are extremely organized and they're risking a lot when their funds are held in escrow, because this is when exit scams happen. As a result, vendors do not hold a lot of money in Darknet vendor accounts, and offer incentives to customers who finalize early.

The Finalizing Early, or FE is another scam that buyers need to be aware of. Finalizing early, means bypassing the escrow system. The vendor(s) are given money directly prior to receiving the product. While this is done frequently with well-known vendors with whom buyers have relationships, scammers often take advantage of this. These scammers will either offer rock bottom prices, or they copy a big Darknet brand name (yes, those exist) and offer only FE sales. Then, they simply collect payments until they're caught and sign up under a new name after being banned. Many scammers make a living like this, without ever sending anything at all.

Many vendor sites are working around this by requiring that vendors pay a security deposit to set up an account. These are the best platforms to use, because it takes the incentive away from the scammers.

## Vetting a Vendor on the Darknet Subreddit

Darknet users can avoid getting taken in by scams by vetting their vendors. Again https://www.reddit.com/r/darknet is the most common place that users turn to check out vendor reputations. Some common warning signs of bad vendors include:

- The vendor is listed in the 'known scammers' section. This is the most obvious, though some vendors have been known to get off this list after improving operations or just changing their names

- Reports of packages never arriving or arriving with fake products

- Reports of vendor being non-responsive or dismissive in messages from buyers

- Reports of vendor trying to run the clock (stall buyer until escrow releases automatically) by offering fake tracking numbers or better deals

- Reports of vendor threatening customers

- Reports of ridiculously below market prices (like Adderall being sold for $10 a pill when they usually go for $20)

Darknet markets attract people who aren't afraid to break the law, or be unethical. Sometimes, people will leave false negative, or positive reviews to control the market. That's why most sites offer vendor stats, which will show the average amount of successful completed transactions and a buyer feedback score. Buyers usually use this score, in conjunction with current comments on Reddit to choose a legitimate vendor.

### The Legal Risk of Darknet Shopping

Generally, the risk when purchasing illegal items from a Darknet vendor is the same as purchasing them in person. Whatever state you're in prevails if you're caught receiving these items by mail. An additional problem that Darknet shopping brings is the federal aspect because sending illegal items in the US mail is a Federal crime.

Many vendors use USPS because it's a government entity. While this seems like a contradiction, it actually gives vendors an additional layer of protection. A US postal worker can't just open a suspicious package. They're required to get a warrant. Generally, for small amounts, this is not worth the trouble. What usually happens instead is that the buyer will get a 'love letter' in their mail, telling them they've received a suspicious item and have X amount of days to come claim it, or it will be incinerated.

Larger amounts will often be reported to authorities, who will determine if it's worth setting up a Controlled Delivery to actually catch the person with the item. Again, it's often not enough for someone to just receive something illegal in the mail, because they have plausible deniability. After all, anyone can send you anything in the mail. This is why law enforcement often attempts to catch the person actually possessing the illegal product to prove they knowingly received drugs in the mail.

The need for this complex investigation often means that small packages of illicit items are much smaller risks than large ones. This is why vendors that can move 'weight' are more desirable than smaller dealers, as they know what to do to avoid getting caught and have a proven track record of moving large amounts to buyers seamlessly

# 6G. - Introduction to Bitcoins

The short answer to the question what is a bitcoin is, in reality, unique lines of code. Bitcoins have no physical body. Essentially, they're nothing more than data, just like the data in your bank account. Financial institutions send and receive this data back and forth as a way of verifying there's actual cash to back up the transaction.

The same thing happens with bitcoins, only it's done between hundreds of different intermediaries, breaking the funds into thousands of pieces of data. So you might buy one bitcoin, but the system will break that bitcoin into thousands of smaller amounts while it's moving from one account to another. The data is reassembled at the end point, before it enters the deposit account as a whole amount again.

The reason for this is anonymity. For someone to find out where that money went, they'd have to follow thousands of strands of code, all going in different directions, which were consistently changed during each point in the transaction, before it reaches its end point. Following that path in either direction is nigh on impossible, and if the bitcoin is purchased with cash, virtually untraceable.

### Economics of Bitcoins

Bitcoins aren't regulated and they have no real financial oversite. As a result, their price fluctuates wildly, based on demand.

When bitcoins first started, they traded on a dollar per dollar basis. As they're pretty much the currency of the Darknet, the Darknet was the financial index through which their value was based. Initially, the price stayed stable.

Then, Ross William Ulbricht got busted for running Silk Road, the Amazon of the Black Market, and demand for them skyrocketed. One month after his arrest, when the Darknet gained mainstream attention, the value of bitcoin skyrocketed to a trading value of 1 to $1216.73 on the Mt. Gox exchange. So while the government might have taken down Ross William Ulbricht, they also turned hundreds of drug dealers into millionaires.

Bitcoin has stabilized slightly since then, now trading at about 1 to $400 as of this writing. Luckily it is possible to purchase pieces of a bitcoin, rather than entire coins.

## How To Buy Bitcoins

Chances are you have a checking account with a debit card. The account is your actual money; the debit card is how you access it. Bitcoins work the same way, in that you'll have the actual bitcoin, and a bitcoin wallet.

Many places that sell bitcoins also offer a bitcoin wallet to hold those funds. One of the oldest, and fastest is Virwox, or the Virtual World Exchange. Virwox doesn't just trade in bitcoins though. They trade in pretty much any common virtual currency, usually used for in game purchases. Virwox is kind of an intermediary between PayPal and bitcoin vendors. See, PayPal doesn't really trust the bitcoin market and as a result, won't allow users to make direct purchases. To get around this, many individuals buy virtual currency through their PayPal account, then trade that virtual currency for bitcoins, all on the same site. While this works, and is the fastest way to buy it, it's also expensive, as you have to pay a lot of transaction fees. However, you will have your wallet and your

bitcoins in one place for ease of use and this is the fastest method.

Coinbase is another exchange that's also a bitcoin wallet, saving you a step. It's a lower cost option, but it can take a bit longer, and you have to use a bank account with it, rather than buy with a credit, debit or PayPal account. Deposits can take several days, unless you have a higher level instant account.

Most sites require that you buy your bitcoins with a bank account, but virtual currency exchanges like Virwox have a way to work around that. Those exchanges work faster, but they usually cost more. The faster you get your bitcoins, the more you have to pay for it.

## What Bitcoins Are Used For

Some think that bitcoins are the currency of the future, while others think they're doomed to fail. There's really no way to predict it, but as long as bitcoins are available, they will always be popular for one thing - buying illegal items on the Darknet. This cryptocurrency is so hard to track that it's the Visa of the Darknet- it's accepted everywhere.

And it's easy to use in Darknet marketplaces. Most sites will offer a Darknet wallet, to hold your bitcoins in to make purchases. It's not recommended that you keep money in them, due to the risks of hacking, but it makes the transfer from your personal wallet to the seller seamless. Most transfers go through within an hour or two of being made.

That's the main use for bitcoins, but some people are making money on literally making money. In order to control the validity of bitcoins, all of the algorithms can be verified through *open source* software. Some individuals within the network will choose to be one of these necessary verification points, through the use of computer software. Their computer tells the other computer the code for the bitcoin is valid, and it moves on through the system. In exchange for providing this service, the individual receives a small amount of bitcoin per transaction. Making thousands of these transactions per day can lead to a huge income. This practice is known as *bitcoin mining*.

## Are Bitcoins Safe?

Probably the biggest question about bitcoins is, are they safe. If you're worried about the legality of it, it's perfectly legal to possess bitcoins, just like any other digital currency. Its ties to the Darknet are what gives the impression of being nefarious.

So while it's not illegal, it should be noted that it's not stable. You could have $400 worth of bitcoins this morning, and have it be worth nothing tomorrow. There's no way to predict the market, or if it will crash. That is why it's recommended that you never hold more bitcoins than you can afford to lose. Buy only the amount you need, and use it quickly. Otherwise, market volatility could have you holding nothing but worthless lines of code.

# 6H. - Darknet Lingo To Know

**Altcoin** – any digital cryptocurrency other than bitcoin

**Bitcoin** – most common cryptocurrency used on the Darknet

**Carding** – the practice of stealing and selling credit card information

**CD** – Controlled Delivery - the technique of controlled delivery is used when drugs are found and allowed to go forward under the control and surveillance of law enforcement officers, usually followed by a raid

**DDOS Attack** – Denial-of-service attack. This attack is used on the Darknet to steal cryptocurrency from admin and user wallets. Can also be the initial sign of an exit scam.

**Direct Buy/Direct Sale** - bypassing a market to work with a vendor using encrypted email and multi-signature escrow

**Dread Pirate Roberts** – the pseudonym used by the administrator of the original Silk Road market, Ross William Ulbricht, commonly shortened to DPR

**Escrow** – On the Darknet, when the administrator holds the Bitcoin for the transaction until the buyer requests payment be made to the seller

**Exit Scam** – when a vendor or market admin decides to shut down business and steal all the bitcoins in their account. With vendors, they usually offer a great deal, leveraging their reputation and gaining as many sales as possible before signing off. Market admins will usually lock user funds before shutting down completely.

**FUD** – Fear, Uncertainty and Doubt, usually used when someone is panicking from not receiving their product for unwarranted reasons.

**FE** – to finalize early or release money to vendor prior to receiving product

**Honest Criminal** – term for a high weight vendor with a solid reputation of delivery, usually not found on marketplaces, but instead transact through direct deals.

**Honeypot** – a hidden service or other website setup by law enforcement in an attempt to attract and trap people who participate in illegal activities.

**LE, LEA, LEO** – Law Enforcement, Law Enforcement Agency, Law Enforcement Organization/Official/Operation

**Love Letter** – an official notice of confiscation from the post office, usually letting the recipient know a suspicious parcel was received and the date the suspicious parcel will be incinerated if the recipient does not arrive to claim it

**Molly** – On the street, it's known as MDMA, but on the Darknet, it's almost always made using other chemicals like ethylone, BZP, a benzofuran, talc, or something potentially toxic like PMA. A common recommendation in Darknet markets is that all Molly purchasers test first with an OTC drug test available in any drugstore.

**Multi Signature Escrow** – where an address is signed by both the buyer and the seller with their private keys. Usually used to move weight, or when doing a direct buy

**Onion** – a hidden website using the Tor network

**P2P Escrow** – Similar to multi-signature escrow, a public key is provided by a seller, market, and vendor, and used to create an address that requires two of the three parties to sign in order to redeem. Usually done when moving significant weight

**Reviews** – the overall feedback left on a site, along with more information gained by outside channels. Used by buyers to determine if they should believe a vendor is legitimate.

**Samples** – in the context of a market, a free or low cost item sent to a well-known buyer in order to establish legitimacy

**Selective Scammer** – a vendor who is known to occasionally scam individuals, but is also known to deliver products (usually to high profile buyers). Typically, victims of selective scamming are new or less Darknet savvy users

**Shilling** – creating accounts on Reddit / Forums for the sole intention of posting Positive / Negative posts about someone or something, trying to make them appear authentic

**Stats** – statistics used to determine legitimacy of buyers/sellers. Most marketplaces make transaction info public to show vendor history to include number of products sold, last online, when established and a numerical value for overall reviews. Usually ranked one to five, with one being poor and 5 being excellent

**Stealth** – the manner of shipping an illegal item

**Weight** – a large amount of illegal drugs, usually marijuana. While there's no set amount, buying 'weight' indicates the person is buying for resale and not personal use.

## 6I. - A Few Words of Warning

While it's not illegal to use Tor, it's illegal to use many of the sites on Tor. Just because you're not buying drugs in the real world doesn't mean you're suddenly floating in international waters. If it's a crime where you live, it's still a crime on the deep web.

In addition, you are not guaranteed anonymity simply by using the deep web. Just like anywhere else, if someone wants to find you bad enough, they'll find you.

Finally, that extra layer of anonymity on Tor will exponentially increase the chance that you're never going to know who you're really talking to. Don't give out personal information, and that includes your personal email. It's best to create a completely separate email, not associated with your real information, for use on Tor and to guard it carefully.

The deep web can be a unique place to discover. Though many of the sites there are nefarious, you can find some interesting things there. Like everywhere else, browse with caution.

For more information on the deep web, check out the Tor site:

https://www.torproject.org/about/overview

# SECTION 4: GLOSSARY, REFERENCES AND SITES OF INTEREST

*People constantly make pop-culture references. That's why it's called popular culture, because people are aware of it and reference it constantly.*

- Seth Rogen, Actor, Comedian, and Author

http://www.brainyquote.com/search_results.html?q=glossary%2C+references

# CHAPTER 7
## Glossary

APPLICATION is a software program or group of programs intended for end users. Often broken down into two classes as either (operating) systems software or application software. Word processing programs, graphics, spreadsheets and games are all applications.

ASP is an Application Service Provider, a type of IT services company who offers hosting of software applications to a wide range of customers for an on-going fee. This enables small companies to outsource many of their IT requirements and alleviates the discomfort of ramping up for new technologies that small businesses struggle with.

BACK-HACK is the use of "electronic bread crumbs" unknowingly left behind in order to determine who hacked into a system.

BEHAVIORAL TARGETING aka BT is when, through sophisticated tracking technology, an online advertiser can put his ad in the readers "path" based on what they've been searching for or viewing recently. Ever wondered why, if you were considering buying new tires, you suddenly have an abundance of ads relating to tires showing up on your screens.

BOTS are part of a network of infected machines called "Botnets." While similar to Trojans and worms, they sneak onto unprotected computers by email from an already infected computer, downloaded by a Trojan or installed by a malevolent website.

BROWSER is a type of software that helps you see, hear, find, and record material on the World Wide Web. Popular browsers include Microsoft Internet Explorer, Mozilla Firefox, Apple Safari, Google Chrome, and others.

BYTES refer to a unit of storage known as binary term- able to hold a single character. Large amounts of memory are indicated by kilobytes (1,024 bytes,) megabytes (1,048,576 bytes,) and gigabytes (1,073,741,824 bytes.)

BSP is a Business Service Provider, a new type of software developer that rents out applications vs. requiring the customer to purchase. One example is ADP, Automatic Data Processing, who provides payroll services.

CATFISH is an online person who pretends to be someone else. The term was coined from the 2010 documentary of the same name, created by Henry Joost, Ariel Schulman and Nev Schulman.

CD stands for compact disc. You may see CDROM (Read Only Memory) and CD-R (Recordable) CD-RW (Re-writable.) You may see them with + or with – signs before the R or RW. (For more detailed information about compact discs, you might want to check out Andy McFadden's www.cdrfaq.org)

CHAT ROOM is a method of communicating with other users in "real time" vs. delayed time, as with email. Chat rooms exist for a huge variety of topics and admission is generally open to anyone. Your comment appears to everyone in the chat room so you don't know who will read or respond to the messages. Caution is in order here.

CPU is the central processing unit of the computer, and is the brain of the computer that helps it carry out orders from programs.

CYBERCRIME is online fraud. Cybercriminals use bots, Trojan horses and spyware to attack.

CYBERSPACE refers to the electronic areas, communities and the culture on computer networks, like the Internet.

DARKNET is the area of the unsearchable Internet where criminal activities occur. This term is often used interchangeably with DEEPWEB.

DEEPWEB is the unsearchable portion of the Internet, estimated to be 500 times bigger than the surface Internet.

DVD stands for digital versatile disc.

DNS means Domain Name Server, introduced in 1984 to permit individual domain names.

EMAIL stand for electronic mail sent from one computer user to another. E-mail may contain word based messages, attachments like photographs, or reports and other forms of multimedia. You must have a modem from an ISP or Internet Service Provider.

FAQ stands for Frequently Asked Questions. Many websites have an FAQ page – often invaluable. Depending on the site, many common questions are addressed on these pages, streamlining the information process.

FORUM (WEB) an online meeting place or online community for exchanging points of view.

HARDWARE refers to the nuts and bolts of equipment, the computer processor, monitor and other peripherals like scanners and printers.

HOME PAGE while often used as the default page for the browser you are using, it is also the introductory or first page of a website owned by a business, individual or organization.

HTML means hypertext mark-up language. This is a document format for the World Wide Web. Text must be converted to HTML to be readable on the web.

HYPERLINK is one or more words, highlighted and underlined in text on the screen. Clicking on a hyperlink takes you directly to another source of information. Sometimes, this hyperlink opens in a new window; sometimes you are taken from the webpage you were on to the linked one.

INFORMATION SUPERHIGHWAY a term coined by Al Gore to represent a global, high speed network of computers serving millions of users simultaneously, transmitting e-mail, voice, video and other multimedia. This system links schools, hospitals, business and government around the world. The U.S. Government's official term for this is "National Information Infrastructure" or NII.

INTERNET the largest computer network in the world.

INTERNET SERVICE PROVIDER (ISP) is a generic term for a provider connecting a user to the Internet, usually for a fee. Recognizable ISPs include America Online (AOL) Yahoo!, Google, and Earthlink to name a few.

MALWARE a category of malicious code that includes worms, viruses, and Trojan Horses seeks to remain undetected on your system.

MEMORY is your computer's hard drive storage, often confused with RAM.

MODEM is a device that permits computers to communicate with other computers over telephone or cable lines and other delivery systems. Modems come in different speeds: the higher the speed, the faster the connection. "Dial-up" uses telephone lines and is typically the slowest connection speed.

MOUSE is the small device connected by a cord to your computer allowing you to give commands to the computer. There are many different kinds available.

MULTIMEDIA refers to a combination of two or more information types like text and images, video and audio.

NET is shortened version of Internet.

NETIQUETTE stands for good manners on the Internet or in cyberspace. Netiquette is "enforced" by other users.

OFFLINE means working on your computer doing things like word-processing while you are not connected to the Internet.

ONLINE any and all activities performed while connected to the Internet.

OS is Operating System (Example: Microsoft's Windows or Apple's Macintosh or Mac).

ORGANIC SEARCH is a means of gaining page views by strategically using keywords and other options to improve a site's ranking in search engine search results.

PASSWORD a confidential word or series of alpha numeric characters that permits access to sites. This is usually used in conjunction with your email address or a User ID.

PC stands for personal computer. Initially combined with IBM as in IBM PC or IBM compatible personal computers or Intel-compatible personal computers. This excludes other types of personal computers like Mac.

PHISHING is an online con game by technologically knowledgeable con artists and identity thieves. It can be in the form of an instant message, spam, e-mail or hateful website and tricks people into revealing sensitive information like credit card numbers or banking information. Phishing attempts often come with a warning that prompts the user to respond, such as your membership will be revoked, or your account suspended. In the body of the phishing email will be a hyperlink. DON'T click on it. The link will transport you to what appears to be the legitimate site. You'll be instructed to provide personal info like a Social Security, credit card or bank account numbers, etc. NOTE: established, legitimate firms will not contact you in this manner. *The author has experienced this numerous times with a sender pretending to be from Paypal.* I immediately send these to: spoof@paypal.com ("If you believe you've received a phishing email, follow these steps right away: Forward the entire email to spoof@paypal.com. Do not alter the subject line or forward the message as an attachment. Delete the suspicious email from your inbox.")

PORTAL (WEB) often called a gateway or entrance to the World Wide Web or some other large online community.

POST is adding information to a forum, your blog, etc.

RAM is Random Access Memory, your computer's temporary memory storage.

SEARCH ENGINE is a program that performs Internet searches based on criteria the user provides. AN example is the Google search engine.

SERVER is a host computer that stores information and software programs that may be accessed by users of other computers.

SOCIAL ENGINEERING is a psychological process where an individual uses fear or scarcity to get a person to give out their private, personal information. This is often used in conjunction with phishing.

SOFTWARE refers to instructions for use on your hardware. There are many types of software. Application software is used to do word processing (MS Word) or to play games while Operating System software is required to run the computer itself. (Windows or MAC) Today, software can be preinstalled on a computer, downloaded or might be on a CD.

SPAM is unwanted e-mail sent to our inbox (often without an address in the TO or CC fields and sent to a large number of recipients) which should be deleted immediately. It is a security concern and a vehicle for sending malware, spyware, and focused phishing attempts.

SPYWARE seeks to remain undetected and can be downloaded from instant messaging, e-mail messages, file sharing connections and even when accepting End User License Agreements from software programs.

TROJAN HORSE is malware that is usually dropped from websites.

TROLL/TROLLING is when an Internet user behaves in an offensive way in a public forum in order to gain attention and start controversy.

URL stands for Uniform Resources Locator. This is an address of a site on the Internet. Example: http://www.AgelessInternet.com.

USERID or USER ID the name you choose to log on with. Many sites require you to pick a User ID before proceeding to download or access information from them. This is especially true of sites where you can make purchases or those to which you pay a fee to belong. (Example: eBay Auctions or ConsumerReports.Org).

VIRTUAL (as in "virtual reality") an artificial environment created with software that provides the user with an experience that persuades him he is truly experiencing reality—a simulated environment created for educational purposes or an imagined one for a game or interactive story.

VPN is a virtual private network which hides your computers IP address.

VIRUS is malware that infects downloaded files.

WEB short for World Wide Web.

WEB SITES are locations on the World Wide Web that may provide basic information or be very interactive with graphics, sounds, shopping carts, and links to other sites. The address will begin with three "w's" www.AgelessInternet.com or may appear as a complete URL (see above).

WORM is malware that is often sent through email and instant messages.

WWW stands for World Wide Web, an HTML based navigation system that must conform to universal standards, permitting most browsers access to a variety of linked resources on the Internet.

*There are a number of resources to consult if you're interested in expanding your Internet terminology such as Netlingo.com and TechTerms.com.* (This section would go on indefinitely, as would the next, if I didn't exercise some restraint .)

# CHAPTER 8
## Links of Interest

This final chapter is intended as a resource to quickly find some of the more useful links on the Internet. Please note that due to the ever changing nature of the Internet, there is a good possibility that not all of them will be in service.

### ANCESTRY (sites for locating info about your family history)

Ancestry.com - http://www.ancestry.com

National Archives - http://www.archives.gov/

### COMPUTING (information on computers and technology tutorials)

Apple Home Page - http://www.apple.com

Code Academy - https://www.codecademy.com/

Electronic Frontier Foundation - http://www.eff.org

Hack this Site! - https://www.hackthissite.org/

Hacking Tutorial Tips & Tricks - http://www.hacking-tutorial.com/

Microsoft Homepage - http://www.microsoft.com

Professor Teaches - http://www.professorteaches.com

## DICTIONARY / THESAURUS (basic helpful programs for looking up words and improving your writing)

Cambridge Dictionary - http://dictionary.cambridge.org/

Grammar Girl - http://www.quickanddirtytips.com/grammar-girl

Merriam Webster Dictionary - http://www.merriam-webster.com

Net Dictionary - http://www.netdictionary.com/

Oxford Dictionary - http://oxforddictionaries.com/

Rhyme Zone Rhyming Dictionary - http://www.rhymezone.com/

Thesaurus.com - http://www.thesaurus.com/

## DRIVING DIRECTIONS & MAPS (driving, walking directions and bus routes when available)

Google Maps - http://www.maps.google.com Google Maps

Map Quest - http://www.mapquest.com

Maps.com - http://www.maps.com

## E-CARDS/ECARDS (Electronic cards and online postcards)

123 Greetings - http://www.123greetings.com/

Angel Winks - http://www.angelwinks.net

Blue Mountain - http://www.bluemountain.com

Care 2 eCards - http://www.care2.com/ecards

Jacquie Lawson Greetings - http://www.jacquielawson.com

Smile Box - http://www.smilebox.com

## EDUCATION (online tutorials and education resources)

About.com - http://www.about.com

American Council on Education - http://www.acenet.edu

The Free Dictionary - http://www.thefreedictionary.com/education

National Center for Education Statistics - http://www.nces.ed.gov

Sylvan Learning Center - http://www.sylvanlearning.com

Udemy – http://www.udemy.com

US Department of Education - http://www.ed.gov

Webopedia - http://www.webopedia.com

Wikipedia - http://www.wikipedia.org

## FINANCE & INVESTING (advice and information on financial markets)

CNN – Money - http://money.cnn.com/

Forbes - http://www.forbes.com

Kiplinger - http://www.kiplinger.com

The Motley Fool - http://www.fool.com

The Wall Street Journal - http://online.wsj.com/home-page/

World Bank - http://www.worldbank.org/

## FUN AND ENTERTAINMENT (joke sites and entertainment sites)

2 Connecting Bloggers - http://www.2leep.com

419 Eater - http://www.419eater.com/

All Recipes - http://www.allrecipes.com

Big Fish Games - http://www.bigfishgames.com/

Bored.com - http://www.bored.com

Cheezburger.com - http://www.cheezburger.com/

Contemporary Art Daily - http://www.contemporaryartdaily.com/

Cracked - http://www.cracked.com/

Despair Inc. - http://www.despair.com

Drew Curtis' FARK - http://www.fark.com

Funny or Die - http://www.funnyordie.com/

Free Online Tarot - http://www.facade.com/

The History Channel - http://www.historychannel.com

Nascar Official Website - http://www.nascar.com

National Geographic http://www.nationalgeographic.com

The Onion - http://www.theonion.com/

PopCap Games - http://www.popcapgames.com

WonderHowTo - http://www.wonderhowto.com/

## GOVERNMENT SITES (official sites for US government organizations)

Center for Disease Control - http://www.cdc.gov

Health Insurance Portal - http://www.healthfinder.gov

House of Representatives - http://www.house.gov

Medicare Official Site - http://www.medicare.gov/

Medicare Online Management - http://my.medicare.gov/

NASA - http://www.nasa.gov

National Institute of Health - http://www.nih.gov

The Office of Disease Prevention and Health Promotion - http://www.health.gov

Senate - http://www.senate.gov

Social Security Administration - http://www.ssa.gov

White House - http://www.whitehouse.gov

## HEALTH & MEDICAL RELATED SITES (sites for insurance and health resources)

Andrew Saul – Doctor Yourself

Hopkins Medicine - http://www.hopkinsmedicine.org

Mayo Clinic - http://www.mayoclinic.com

Web MD - http://www.webmd.com

The World Health Organization - http://www.who.int

## JOB- RELATED (sites for career planning and finding jobs)

Careerbuilder – http://www.careerbuilder.com

Career One Stop - http://www.careeronestop.org/jobsearch/findjobs/state-job-banks.aspx

Corn on the Job - http://www.cornonthejob.com/

Indeed – http://www.indeed.com

Job Jenny - http://www.jobjenny.com/

Life After College - http://www.lifeaftercollege.org/

LinkedIn – http://www.linkedin.com

Monster.com - http://www.monster.com/

Seniors for Hire - http://www.seniors4hire.org

Wise Worker - http://www.wiserworker.com

## MUSEUMS (famous museum sites, many include virtual tours)

American Museum of Natural History - http://www.amnh.org

J. Paul Getty Museum - http://www.getty.edu/museum

Louvre - http://www.louvre.fr

Museum of Fine Arts in Boston - http://www.mfa.org

Museum of Light - http://www.museumoflight.org

The Museum of Science and Industry - http://www.msichicago.org

Smithsonian - http://www.si.edu

## NETIQUETTE (Net Etiquette)

Netiquette Guidelines - http://tools.ietf.org/html/rfc1855

Netiquette Home Page - http://www.albion.com/netiquette

Net Manners - http://www.netmanners.com/

Stop Cyber Bullying - http://www.stopcyberbullying.org/kids/msparrysguidetonetiquette.html

PETS and ANIMALS (sites for pet lovers and people seeking info on their pets)

American Cat Fanciers Association - http://www.acfacat.com

American Kennel Club - http://www.akc.org

Cat Fanciers Association - http://www.cfa.org

Cute Overload - http://cuteoverload.com

Pet Finder - https://www.petfinder.com/

Pet Health - http://www.pethealth.org

Pet Loss - http://www.petloss.com

Pet MD - http://www.petsmd.com

Rainbow Bridge - http://www.rainbowbridge.org

REFERENCE SITES (sites for getting information on just about everything)

Better Business Bureau - http://www.bbb/org/us

Charity Watch - http://www.charitywatch.org

CNet Reviews - http://reviews.cnet.com

Consumer Reports - http://www.consumerreports.org/

PC Magazine - http://www.pcmag.com

Pew Research Center - http://www.pewInternet.org/

Rand Corporation - http://www.rand.org

## SOCIAL NETWORKING/ONLINE DATING (sites for friends and more)

420 Dating - http://420dating.org//

Clown Dating - http://www.clowndating.com/

eHarmony - http://www.eharmony.com

Match.com - http://www.match.com/

Meet an Inmate - http://www.meet-an-inmate.com/

OK Cupid - https://www.okcupid.com/

Our Time – http://www.ourtime.com

Plenty of Fish - http://www.pof.com/

Punk Match - http://www.punkmatch.com/

Zoosk - http://www.zoosk.com

## TRAVEL (sites for planning vacations and coming up with vacation ideas)

Kayak - http://www.kayak.com/

Orbitz - http://www.orbitz.com

Priceline - http://www.priceline.com

Rand McNally - http://www.randmcnally.com

Roadside America - http://www.roadsideamerica.com

Transitions Abroad - http://www.transitionsabroad.com/listings/travel/sen ior/index.shtml

Travel - http://www.travel.com

Trip Advisor - http://www.tripadvisor.com

## WEATHER (local, regional and weather news)

Farmer's Almanac - http://farmersalmanac.com/

Intellicast - http://www.intellicast.com/Local/

National Weather Service - http://www.weather.gov

Weather.org - http://www.weather.org

The Weather Channel - http://www.weather.com

Weather Underground - http://www.wunderground.com

I hope you've found this information of value. Your feedback is welcome. Please drop me a line at comments@TheStraightforwardInternet.com.

*~To Your Safe & Exhilarating Internet Exploration – Terry Lynne Hale*

# CHAPTER 9
## The End of the Journey

Thank you for taking the time to read this. I hope you found this reference guide helpful. Of course, in the exciting and ever changing cyber universe, things are always changing and new things are always being discovered. Not only will there be billions of Internet connected things in the world ten years from now, some of them haven't been invented yet.

They haven't even been imagined yet.

It only takes one piece of technology to change the way we look at everything. From CPUs that could fit in a shoebox, to iPhones that changed the way we use our phones, it only takes one big idea to change the entire world again.

The digital universe is seeping into our everyday lives all the time. It's no longer just a place for techno geeks. Instead, it's a world for all of us, no matter what our level of ability. Whether you can barely use email, or you're an expert on the deep web, we're all connected via this invisible universe. Take advantage of it.

And on a final note, I'll leave you with two quotes that really resonate with me:

*You don't learn to walk by following rules. You learn by doing and by falling over.*

- Richard Branson

http://www.brainyquote.com/quotes/quotes/r/richardbra414117.html

*and*

*Live as if you were to die tomorrow. Learn as if you were to live forever.*

- Mahatma Gandhi

http://www.brainyquote.com/quotes/quotes/m/mahatmagan133995.html

# ABOUT THE AUTHOR

**Terry Lynne Hale** is a Kansas City author and freelance writer with extensive business experience in sales, marketing and training. A relentless quest for learning led her to explore the WWW after buying her first PC in 1995. Naturally, she wanted to share her enthusiasm for the Internet with others. Her training and writing background fueled the passion that led her to write and publish her first book, *Ageless Internet*. Following the success of that award- winning first book, she moved onto the second aimed at Gen-X and all others who enjoy learning as she does. You can read updates on her blog, Terry Lynne's Take, at http://www.TerryLynneHale.com.

Author cover photo by Bliss Photography

# REFERENCES
## (Endnotes)

1   Rivera, Janessa, and Muelen, Robert. "Gartner Says 4.9 Billion Connected "Things" Will Be in Use in 2015." *Gartner*. 11 Nov. 2014. <http://www.gartner.com/newsroom/id/2905717>.

2   "Usage and Population Statistics." *Internet World Stats*. <http://www.Internetworldstats.com/>.

3   "Online Dating Statistics." *Statistic Brain*. <http://www.statisticbrain.com/online-dating-statistics/>.

4   Kessler, Sarah. "3% Of Americans Still Use Dial-Up Internet." *Fast Company*. 26 Aug. 2013. <http://www.fastcompany.com/3016298/3-of-americans-still-use-dial-up-Internet>.

5   Rosoff, Matt. "People Either Check Email All the Time, or Barely at All." *Business Insider*. Business Insider, Inc, 17 Aug. 2015. <http://www.businessinsider.com/how-often-do-people-check-their-email-2015-8>.

6   "The Man Who Made You Put Away Your Pen." *NPR*. NPR, 21 Nov. 2009. <http://www.npr.org/templates/story/story.php?storyId=120364591>.

7   "Email Client Marketshare and Popularity." *Campaign Monitor*. <https://www.campaign-monitor.com/dev-resources/will-it-work/email-clients/>.

8   "Most Used Instant Messaging Apps 2015 | Statistic." *Statista*. <http://www.statista.com/statistics/258749/most-popular-global-mobile-messenger-apps/>

9    Crook, Jordan, and Anna Escher. "A Brief History Of Snapchat.» *TechCrunch*. <http://techcrunch.com/gallery/a-brief-history-of-snapchat/slide/8/>.

10   "Burundanga." *Snopes*. <http://www.snopes.com/crime/warnings/burundanga.asp>.

11   "No. 1 Position in Google Gets 33% of Search Traffic." *Search Engine Watch*. <http://searchenginewatch.com/sew/study/2276184/no-1-position-in-google-gets-33-of-search-traffic-study>

12   "Top 20 Facebook Statistics." *Zephoria*. 2015, October 18. <https://zephoria.com/top-15-valuable-facebook-statistics/>

13   "Twitter Usage Statistics." *Internet Live Stats*. <http://www.Internetlivestats.com/twitter-statistics/>

14   "Demographics of Key Social Networking Platforms." *Pew Internet*. 2015, January 9. <http://www.pewInternet.org/2015/01/09/demographics-of-key-social-networking-platforms-2/>

15   25 LinkedIn Facts and Statistics for 2015. (n.d.). Retrieved November 16, 2015, from http://www.sensiblemarketing.com/blog/25-linkedin-facts-and-statistics-for-2015

16   "Statistics." *Youtube*. <https://www.youtube.com/yt/press/statistics.html>

17   "150 Amazing Instagram Statistics." *Expanded Ramblings*. 2014, March 6. <http://expandedramblings.com/index.php/important-instagram-stats/>

18   Epstein, Zach. "How to find the Invisible Internet." *BGR*. 2014, January 20. <http://bgr.com/2014/01/20/how-to-access-tor-silk-road-deep-web/>

19   "Freenet - Overview." *Freenet Project*. <https://freenetproject.org/>

# INDEX

## A

# B

# C

# D

## I

## J

## K

## L

# T

# U

uBid.com, 47
Udemy, 77
Ulbricht, Ross William, 59–60, 63, 64
Uniform Resources Locator (URL), 73
Unite (keyboards and mice), 26

United States Postal Service (USPS), 62
uploading, 7
US Department of Education, 77
us.ebid.net, 47
Userid/User ID, 73

# V

vendors, vetting, 61
Viber, 13
video chats, 13
video hosting websites, 37
video players, 24
videos, tutorial, 54
View Sonic, 27
violence porn websites, 45
virtual, defined, 73
virtual private networks (VPNs), 54–55, 73
virtual reality, 36

virtual storage, 25, 35
Virtual World Exchange, 63
viruses
    avoiding, 17
    defined, 74
    scan programs, 7, 28
    spreading, 27–28
    symptoms, 31
Virwox (bitcoin wallet), 63
VPNs (virtual private networks), 54–55, 73

# W

The Wall Street Journal, 77
We Be High website, 45
The Weather Channel, 83
Weather Underground, 83
weather websites, 83
Weather.org, 83
web (World Wide Web), 74
Web MD, 79
webcams, 26–27
WeBidz.com, 47
Webopedia, 77
Webroot, 29
websites, 74
    . See also specific sites by name
WebStore.com, 47
WeChat, 13

weight, illegal drugs, 61
WhatsApp, 13
White House website, 79
Wi-Fi (wireless Internet service), 8, 9
Wikipedia, 77
Wikipedia (Easter Egg), 41, 42
Windows Live Desktop, 11
WinZip, 52
wireless Internet service (Wi-Fi), 8, 9
wireless protocols, 8
Wise Worker website, 80
WiTopia, VPN service, 55
WonderHowTo, 78
WordPress, 6, 38
work, use of Internet, 6, 37
World Bank, 77

www.ingramcontent.com/pod-product-compliance
Lightning Source LLC
Chambersburg PA
CBHW080557060326
40689CB00021B/4882

*9780692703731*